From Beans to Brew

The Ultimate Guide to Starting and

Running a Successful Café

Sarah Watson

Published by Elf Law Pty Ltd, Brisbane, Australia.

ISBN: 978-0-6458852-5-5 (e-book)

ISBN: 979-8-8655010-6-0 (paperback)

Cover design by Elizabeth Murray.

This publication is designed to provide accurate and authoritative information in regard to the subject matter covered. It is sold with the understanding that the author and the publisher are not engaged in rendering legal, business, financial, accounting or other professional services. If legal advice or other expert assistance is required, the services of a competent professional person should be sought.

There will never be a right time.

Stop waiting and start doing.

- Mel Robbins

Introduction

Did you know that coffee is second only to water as the beverage of choice in the United States? Six out of ten people drink coffee every single day, translating to over 400 million cups of coffee per day![1]

With 1 billion coffee drinkers worldwide drinking an average of 2 billion cups daily[2], it's safe to say coffee is not going anywhere anytime soon. A large reason for this is the vibrant coffee culture.

People love coffee, and they've integrated it into every aspect of their lives, from pick-me-ups to workplace coffee breaks to coffee dates. It is an acceptable social beverage.

This is what makes starting a café so exciting and rewarding! The market is there, and if you play your cards right, you can unlock your creativity and transform your café into the go-to social hub.

This book will teach you how to do that, from creating your café vision to delivering an outstanding customer experience and everything you need to know about starting and running a profitable café.

In **Chapter 1**, we'll work through creating your vision, a foundational building block of a successful café.

Chapter 2 dives into the importance of a well-thought-out business plan.

Chapter 3 examines the importance of finding the right location and setting yourself up for success in landlord negotiations.

---

[1] https://pubmed.ncbi.nlm.nih.gov/35578955/
[2] https://britishcoffeeassociation.org/coffee-facts/

Chapter 4 works through creating your brand – image, culture and identity.

Chapter 5 covers the perfect menu, the importance of aligning your menu with your brand and the need to make a profit.

In **Chapter 6**, we set out the essential supplies to ensure everything runs smoothly on opening day.

Your team is the focus of **Chapter 7**, with the importance of hiring the right team to fit your café's culture and vision.

Chapter 8 delves into the legal and regulatory requirements to ensure your café is compliant from day one.

In **Chapter 9**, we work through marketing and promotional strategies specific to cafés.

Finally, **Chapter 10** covers the importance of delivering an outstanding customer experience – first time and every time.

You will find that some of the legal and regulatory requirements mentioned in Chapter 8 refer to departments and forms in the United States of America. Each country will have legal and regulatory requirements for small business ownership, which will be relevant, and it is essential that you find out what your local requirements are. Regardless, the themes regarding compliance in this Chapter are relevant wherever you are setting up your new cafe.

One last thing before you get started – if you are looking for a way to work through each of the steps in this café journey you can pick up the Beans to Brew Companion Workbook. The Companion Workbook walks you through each of the chapters in this book with exercises and prompts for you to map out your café journey.

You can find the Companion Workbook here

https://www.amazon.com/Beans-Brew-Companion-Workbook-Successful/dp/B0CWHCHPRT

So, what are you waiting for?

Let's get started!

Table of Contents

Chapter 1: Finding Your Cafe Vision 1

Define The Concept And Theme Of Your Café...............................1

Identify Your Target Market 6

Research The Local Market..................................8

Create A Unique Selling Proposition For Your Café 10

Chapter 2: Planning Your Café Business 13

The Importance of A Well-Structured Business Plan 13

Outlining The Different Sections of The Business Plan 16

Chapter 3: Location, Location, Location 23

Your Café's Location 23

Factors to Consider When Selecting a Suitable Site 24

Negotiating Leases And Dealing With Landlords........................... 29

Chapter 4: Crafting Your Cafe's Brand...............................33

Build A Strong And Memorable Brand Identity 35

Develop Your Brand Image... 37

Create Your Brand Culture..38

Cultivate Your Brand Personality.....................................39

Chapter 5: The Perfect Menu... 43

Design a Menu that Complements Your Café's Concept................. 43

Select High-Quality Ingredients 44

Incorporate Diversity for Different Dietary Preferences................. 47

Price Your Products for Profitability.................................50

Chapter 6: Essential Equipment and Supplies....................53

Identify the Necessary Café Equipment and Tools........................53

Assess the Right Balance Between Affordability and Quality.........59

Understand the Importance of Efficient Workflow in the Kitchen.60

Manage Inventory and Order Supplies Effectively.........................63

Chapter 7: Recruiting and Managing Your Team.................67

Hire the Right People to Fit Your Cafe's Culture and Vision..........67

Train Employees for Exceptional Customer Service.......................70

Create a Positive Work Environment and Foster Teamwork..........72

Handle HR Responsibilities and Employee Retention....................75

Chapter 8: Navigating Legal and Regulatory Requirements 81

Obtain the Necessary Permits and Licenses....................................81

Understand Food Safety and Health Regulations...........................82

Compliance with Employment Laws and Workplace Safety...........84

Chapter 9: Marketing and Promotion Strategies.................91

Develop a Comprehensive Marketing Plan for Your Café...............91

Harness The Power of Social Media and Online Presence..............92

Engage in Local Community Events and Partnerships...................94

Utilize Loyalty Programs and Customer Retention Techniques.....96

Chapter 10: Delivering an Outstanding Customer Experience
....103

Cultivate a Welcoming Atmosphere and Ambiance......................103

Enhance Customer Service and Handling Feedback 104

Implement Effective Customer Engagement Strategies 107

Conclusion **115**

A note from the Author **117**

Appendix: **119**

Cafe Business Plan Worksheet 119

Checklist for Opening Day Preparations 123

Resource List for Further Reading and Research 127

Chapter 1: Finding Your Cafe Vision

One thing I've learned as a café owner is that it is easy to want to do it all and do it as soon as possible when you're starting a café. This is because customers want what they want, and as a new café owner, you want to deliver to build your customer base. And if you do that, you'll find yourself ragged, trying to fulfill every order and embracing every suggestion thrown your way. You cannot be all things to all people – well you can, but it doesn't usually end well.

But,

That's not how to run any business; you need a vision to succeed.

A vision helps you plan your business strategically and grow it as needed. Think of your vision as you would a vehicle that's meant to lead you to success. If you tell everyone where you're going and what route you'll take, you'll be better positioned to utilize your resources wisely. But if you let others dictate your route, you may over-extend your budget, buy equipment you'll hardly use, and hire people you can't afford to pay to keep your customers happy.

That's a surefire way to become a miserable café owner.

So, what do you need to do?

Define The Concept And Theme Of Your Café

You should **ask yourself what you want your café to be known for**. If your answer is coffee, your vision is too general. It would be best if you had a more nuanced answer; to get it, you have to define the concept and theme of your café.

Developing a concept is essential for:

- Creating your brand identity

- Tailoring your business to your target audience. This includes your menu, décor, and how you'll market your café.

- Developing your menu and pricing it

- Creating a suitable atmosphere. For instance, the atmosphere can be intimate, cozy, or trendy.

- Consistency – Your concept acts as your guide. It helps you maintain consistency regarding the menu, branding, and the atmosphere you want to create.

So, how can you figure out your concept?

Start by *doing a mental walk through your café*.

Let's say you're standing at the door of your café; what do you see? As you walk inside, what do you notice? Picture yourself designing the interior of your café from top to bottom. As you're doing so, what drives you? That's the concept of your café.

Your concept can be driven by:

- *Something you're passionate about*. For instance, if you love cosplay, all things retro or rock music, you may choose to center your theme on that passion. That way, your staff and your customers can connect with you, dress in a particular way, enjoy particular music with you.

- **The need to fill a gap**: If you intend to fill a gap in your community or serve a specific market, your café must show that. For instance, if you allow pets in your café, you'll make it easier for customers to come in with their pets.

- **Serving your community**: You can think of what your community needs and create a café to serve that need. For instance, if your community needs a place to meet up, you can start your café with that in mind.

- **Creating your legacy:** If you wish to build a family business that can serve as a long-lasting legacy for you and your family, you need to find ways to leave your mark so the community can familiarize themselves with who you are. For instance, it may be that you have a unique family recipe or a family history with a love affair with coffee – think about how you can incorporate those themes into daily life at your café.

As you can see, your café's concept will impact the layout of your café, the décor, the menu, and the conduct of your staff. Thus, take your time to develop your concept. Visit other cafés, talk to industry experts, do your market research, and collaborate with other professionals to develop your concept. For instance, you can talk to designers, marketing experts, and even chefs to discover what sells and what you can offer your potential customers.

With that said, there are five things you should never forget when theming a café. These are:

- **The User Experience**

While you can adopt a specific concept you're passionate about when starting your café, you must also consider the user experience when implementing your ideas. Let's take the example of the pet-friendly café. It's one thing to say you allow pets into your establishment but another thing to ensure that all your customers and their pets have a great experience while visiting your café.

The same goes for any other theme you want to focus on. Let's say you want to start a café that caters to writers. You need to ask yourself what writers need to do their work and provide it to them. In this instance, you can provide Wi-Fi and a comfortable desk or table to enable them to work.

In other words, you should be able to back up your café's concept and theme by making it easier for your customers to enjoy the things promised.

- **The Selling Point**

Your café is a business. So, whatever theme you decide on should be tied to your selling point. You don't want people to come in, admire your décor, use your internet, and leave without buying anything. Tie your theme to what you want to sell. For instance, if your café is centered on unique flavors, those flavors should be on the menu and well-displayed for all to see. You can offer discounts or coupons or dedicate certain days to the things you want to sell.

- **The Atmosphere**

For your idea to work, you need to get your customers excited about the café's interior, the atmosphere, and your products. Make them see what

4

you offer, create an atmosphere that goes well with the theme, and excite them about trying your products.

Let's say your café is big on classic television shows. It would be best if you created an atmosphere that elevates the characters. For example, you can have wax figures of the characters, a Hall of Fame board with photos and important dates, and replicas of what the atmosphere entails. Also, have menus dedicated to the characters. Anyone walking into the café should be able to sense the significance of the display even if they don't know much about the characters.

- **The Ease of Purchase**

As you design your café according to your vision, you must remember that ***the end goal is selling your products***. This means you should make it easy for them to do so. If you are selling various products and merchandise, consider the ease of purchase. If you make it hard for your customers to purchase stuff, they will not buy things, not because they don't want to but because it is bothersome.

A good way to ensure ease of purchase is to go through the process yourself and get 'test customers' to assess the process. Try thinking of different scenarios. For instance, you can pretend to be customer number 10, 20, or 30, waiting in line. Look at your processes from that customer's point of view. If you're waiting in line, what are you doing then? What are you seeing? How long are you waiting for?

And when you get to the front, how is the service? Can you quickly pay for your purchases using your café's various options?

- **Value Addition**

If you have a great concept, why not make the most of it?

You can do this by adding value to your products. If you want to cater to writers, give them the Wi-Fi password. If you want to allow pets in your café, you should have designated places for pets. You can even have a place for toys, pet dishes, and a pet menu. The value you add doesn't have to be big but has to be there.

Review your theme and determine what you can do to make your customers feel they are getting the most out of the experience.

Identify Your Target Market

You cannot imagine what your café will look like without considering who will be visiting your café. It would be best to design your café and its menu to attract your target market. Plus, when you know your target audience, you can develop marketing strategies according to their preferences.

Think of the people you want to sell to in terms of:

- Age

- Gender

- Occupation

- Distance to the café

- Their coffee habits

All these things will impact your café and menu.

But don't make the mistake of thinking that everyone in your target market has the same preferences. Just because someone is a particular gender or age does not mean they like the same things.

Coffee drinkers can be:

- **Caffeine Fiends**

Caffeine fiends drink for the buzz. They want pick-me-ups, and they want it now. As such, they are not too keen about the taste of their coffee as long as it has enough caffeine content to satisfy their craving. Such customers drink instant coffees, dark roast coffees, and coffees that have high caffeine content.

- **Milk Lovers**

Milk lovers enjoy their coffee with milk, cream, and sugar. They want something creamy and sweet and will pay extra for the best milk and cream. Such customers love flavored coffees, creamy coffees, and sweetened coffees.

- **Taste Seekers**

Taste seekers want to explore different flavors of coffee. If something smells excellent and tastes great, they're sold. They can even pay extra to ensure the coffee beans are of the highest quality. Such customers would appreciate artisanal coffees, specialty coffees, and single-origin coffees. And since they want to experience different flavors, they won't be offended by 'bad' coffee. Instead, they'll look forward to the next flavor. So, you need to know how to take advantage of that.

- **Iced Coffee Drinkers**

These are customers who want their coffee cold or iced. They want something cool and refreshing and will pay extra for higher-quality iced coffee. They love iced coffees, nitro cold brews, and cold brew coffees.

This means you'll need to find ways to keep your coffee cold to serve such customers.

As you can see, your target market will affect the type of coffee you want to make, the equipment you buy, your pricing, and your marketing strategy. So, create a profile of your target market; it is a huge part of your café's vision.

Apart from that, some coffee drinkers love sitting down to have their coffee; some prefer their coffee to go or both. Considering such things can help you tailor your business to your target market and increase sales.

Research The Local Market

While it's tempting to focus on your café and believe in your skills and business acumen, you must not forget that the competition will affect your vision. You must do market research to know what you're against.

Some things to consider are:

- How many cafés are in the vicinity?

- Are they franchises or individual brands?

- How many customers do they get?

- When are they busy?

- What time do they open and close?

- What do they sell?

- How many employees do they have?

- How long does it take them to serve customers?

- What does their menu look like?

- What are the customers ordering? What are they saying about the place?

- What are the customers complaining about?

- What do you like or dislike about their café?

- Can you compete with them head-on?

- What's the foot traffic near your café?

The more information you get, the better prepared you'll be to run your own business.

But **caution is advised**.

If you're too focused on what others are doing, you may find yourself going above and beyond to create a café that can compete with them right from the start. But your intention in doing market research is not to copy others. It is to **figure out a gap in the market and what you can do to fill it with the resources you have.**

Remember, copying others for their café design and menu is easy, but you don't know their vision and plan going forward. So, while it is essential to study others, it is equally as important to take what you learn and make it yours.

Apart from visiting various cafés to get firsthand experience about their services, you may want to **conduct surveys and analyze data on** *local trends* to get a clearer view of your potential customers and how to sell to them.

Create A Unique Selling Proposition For Your Café

Your selling proposition is **the slogan you'll use to attract potential customers**. It represents your vision – the concept and theme of your café, and it distinguishes your café from your competitors.

In other words, your selling proposition answers the question, *"Why should we choose you?"*

This step is beneficial because it:

- *Sets your café apart from others*: This makes it easier for you to build your brand.

- *Shifts the focus from the price of your products*: If there's something extra you're offering at your café, your customers won't focus too much on your prices. For instance, if your selling proposition focuses on 'fresh coffee' or your own 'unique blend', customers will focus on that and come to you for that reason.

- *Increases conversion rates*: People are attracted to catchy phrases. They'll enter your café because of your selling proposition.

To develop your selling proposition:

- **Research Your Audience**

If you want to sell to your target market, you need to know what they want and let them know you can provide it. For instance, if they take their coffee black and your slogan is 'sweet and creamy,' chances are they will learn to associate your café with sweetness, and it won't be the first place they think of when they want coffee.

- **Fill a Need**

If there is a need other cafés in your area are not fulfilling, you can take it upon yourself to fulfill that need and include it in your selling proposition. For instance, if your customers love taking photos for Instagram, you can have something like 'world's most Instagrammable café' and then make sure your café's interior is suitable for taking pictures.

- **Find Out What's In Demand**

It's good to find out what your customers are asking for. This way, you can paraphrase and use their words as your selling proposition. For instance, if your customers crave strong coffee, your selling proposition could be "World's strongest coffee." But be careful not to limit your selling proposition too much, or you may discourage some customers from trying your coffee.

- **Keep It Simple**

Your selling proposition should be creative but simple. Your customers should be able to remember your slogan. If they remember it, they will look for your café instead of buying from any other café.

- **Back It Up**

Your selling proposition acts as your word. It is your café's guarantee. Your customers buy from you because they are attracted to what you've promised to give them. As such, you need to find ways to fulfill that promise. For example, if you promise iced coffee, don't serve lukewarm coffee, and expect your customers to be happy. That's not what you guaranteed.

Always remember your vision for your café does not have to be fulfilled in one go. You can start small and then expand your vision as your business grows. But that will take some planning, which we will discuss next.

Chapter 2: Planning Your Café Business

Do you recall the first time you thought of starting a café?

No doubt you had an idea of the type of café you wanted to start, and as you read the first chapter of this book, you learned that your café's concept affects various aspects of your business, so you have to think about it carefully. This is because when it comes down to it, you want a viable business concept, not just any concept.

The birth of your café starts with a concept. But to turn that idea into reality, you need a plan.

The Importance of A Well-Structured Business Plan

A well-structured business plan:

- **Proves the Validity of Your Concept**

The first thing a business plan does is help you see if your business idea is viable. When writing the plan, you will assess market dynamics, research competitors, and develop financial projections.

Such things will help you re-evaluate your goals and develop strategies to help you achieve success.

- **Reduces Potential Risks**

Businesses fail when they fail to:

- *Set enough money aside*: You need to know your startup costs, make a profit and loss forecast, do a break-even analysis, and create a cash flow statement when developing your business plan. This helps you know how long it will take to start making money from your business and how hard you must work until then. Most people ignore this part and find themselves in financial trouble a few months into running their café.

- **Plan for stiff competition**: When you start your café, other people in the vicinity will note what you're doing, and they will not stand by quietly if they perceive your business as a threat to theirs. This often shocks new business owners, especially if they weren't expecting it.

- **Research pricing**: If you don't research pricing, you may end up pricing your products too high or too low. If you price them too high, people will go to your competitors, and if you price them too low, you'll fail to make a profit, and you'll find it hard to raise the prices later on.

- **Do market research**: If you don't research the market, you may fail to realize that your products are not wanted or needed. For instance, you may set up a shop in a sprawling business district without realizing that most of the businesses in the area have signed contracts with particular cafés or coffee delivery services. Or, you may start selling products that people in the area don't use for ethical or religious reasons. That would result in a huge loss.

- **Plan for explosive growth**: What happens when your business achieves overnight success? If you don't plan for such a scenario, you may lose out on the opportunity for growth, draining all your capital or burning out to keep up with demands. On the other hand, you need to weigh any deals you may get with caution. Not every opportunity is a good thing. Stay true to your café's concept and give yourself room to care for your well-being even as you grow your business.

As you can see, **a business plan acts as your roadmap**. It serves as a guide that lets you know how to react in certain situations and thus helps you reduce risk.

- **Helps You Secure Investments**

A business plan lets you know how much money you need to spend on various aspects of your business. Thus, even if you're self-financing, having a good business plan will help you have a realistic view of how much money you need.

But there's something else a good business plan does.

It helps show others that you are serious about starting a café. This makes borrowing money from financial institutions, friends, and family easier. Remember, business investors and financiers love looking at the financial aspect of a business. But they also want to see how you plan to achieve those numbers. So, if you have a business plan, they can note that you've researched, developed a viable product, and outlined your marketing strategy. These are all ingredients for success.

- **Enables You to Plan Purchases and Allocate Resources**

There are things you will need to run and expand your business. For instance, you need to spend cash on:

- Product and service development

- Sales and marketing

- Hiring

- New technology

- Operations

As you write your business plan, you'll first discover that you need to budget for what you need to make profits as soon as possible. If you have the money to buy the latest equipment and hire many people, you might not pay too much attention to how much money you're spending.

A business plan lets you consider what you're doing and where you're spending your money. It enables you to know how much you can spend, where to get the best products, and what you can do to manage your resources effectively. You can also include plans for future products and expansion. This way, you can allocate cash to your plans even as you focus on making your current plan successful.

- **Details Your Marketing Strategy**

When writing a business plan, you have to include your marketing strategy. This strategy aims to detail how you will reach your target market and how you will build brand awareness. Without a marketing strategy, it would be difficult for you to reach your goals.

All in all,

A business plan sets you up for success, so you must write a good plan.

Outlining The Different Sections of The Business Plan

Don't be overwhelmed by the term 'business plan.' Remember, a business plan serves as your map or guide. It is designed to take you from one point to another; you can divide it into sections and tackle one at a time.

Different sections of a business plan include:

- **Executive Summary**

Think of the executive summary as you would a cover letter. Its purpose is to introduce your business. This means you should briefly overview your café business and outline its objectives concisely and engagingly.

- **Company Description**

This is where you talk about your café's mission, business partners, ownership, legal structure, and goals. When listing ownership and business partners, you may want to list any skills, qualifications, training, and experience they may have. Also, note down who owns the majority shares.

When writing your company description, you can also state why you chose that particular business location for your café.

- **Market Analysis**

This part deals with your target market and your competition. You need to list down the characteristics of your target market and give a description of your competitors. The purpose of this section is to show that you have a viable business idea.

- **Products and Services**

This section should list everything you plan on selling and the services you will be providing. For instance, you can have categories such as:

- Breakfast pastries

- Hot drinks

- Cold drinks

- Smoothies

Go into detail when listing the products. For instance, if you sell breakfast pastries, you can name apple crumble tarts, almond croissants, and jam doughnuts.

Apart from listing your products and services, you should also mention competitive advantages and any unique features your café will have.

- **Marketing and Sales Strategy**

This is where you outline what you must do to attract and retain customers. You must include your pricing strategy, advertising and promotion plans, and social media strategy.

- **Operations Plan**

This part of your business plan outlines how you plan to run your café. As such, it should include inventory management, staffing requirements, and other operational considerations.

- **Financial Plan**

The financial plan provides your café's financial information. It includes your startup costs, revenue projections, and profit and loss statements. Potential investors and financiers will be interested in viewing this part of your business plan before deciding if they should invest.

Expected startup costs include:

- Rental space

- Insurance

- Utilities

- Furnishing and equipment

- Licenses and permits

- Staff wages

- Advertising

Your financial plan will help you see how much money you have and how much you can afford to spend on the various startup costs. Thus, you need to calculate your startup costs, operating expenses, and the break-even point.

As part of the plan, *looking at funding options and ways to secure the finances you need for your business would be prudent*. Remember, startup costs depend on various things, including the type of café you want to open, the location of the café, and the local commercial real estate prices. On average, you can spend anywhere from $50,000 to $400,000.

As such, you need to consider where you will get the funds. Some sources of funding you can look into include:

- **Business loans**: Brand new startups do not often qualify for business loans like SBA. But once you operate your café for a few years and show that your business is doing well, you can apply for such loans to expand your business. The trick is to avoid bad financial decisions such as paying your bills late. Pay your credit card debts and bills on time to build your credit score.

- **Business lines of credit**: This is a better funding option for new businesses than the standard business loan. When you use this option, your business gets a set amount of cash from the bank, which you can use to cover your café expenses. The bank will give you a draw period when you can tap into your funds until you reach your credit limit. If you qualify for a business line of credit, you'll need a mobile app, credit card, or checking account to access the funds. Before you select a business line of credit, you need to look at costs such as interest, late fees, annual maintenance fees, and draw fees to determine if it is worth it.

- **Business credit cards:** Business credit cards are similar to your credit card; most are unsecured. They come with fixed limits; you can use the card to purchase some of your requirements or get cash advances. Before getting a business credit card, study fees include interest, over-limit fee, cash advance fee, late fee, and annual fee.

- **Equipment financing**: You should look into equipment financing when starting a café business. This is where you're given money to purchase the equipment you need for your business. The equipment serves as collateral, so this type of funding is easier to qualify for. As a café owner, you must think of the products and hardware you need to run your business before deciding what you can buy outright and what you can seek financing for.

- **Startup funding**: Nowadays, many financial institutions are willing to lend money to startups. For instance, you can seek financing from SBA microloans or apply for business grants. If you choose this type of funding, you must review the stipulations carefully. Read the fine print before making your decision.

- **_Self-funding_**: You don't have to borrow all the money you need to start a business. You can save up to fund your business. This may mean saving some cash before you can start your café. If you take this route, place your money in a high-yield savings account to continue generating interest until you're ready to use it.

As you make your financial plan, **_you must not forget to consider things such as seasonality and price fluctuations._** There are times when the products and equipment you want are cheaper and times when they are more expensive. Thus, plan accordingly.

Also, it is good to point out that the price of starting a business may go up as time goes by. Thus, your current prices may go up in a few years. Therefore, you have to act once you make your plan.

- **Appendices**

This is where you include any other relevant information. It can consist of things such as:

- Support documentation, including charts, graphs, or tables, that provide relevant information regarding your business

- Vendor or client contracts and agreements

- Licenses, permits, trademarks, and patent documentation

- Resumes for those involved in the business

- Detailed market studies

- Building permit

- Equipment lease documentation

- Marketing materials

- Contact information for accountants, advisors, and attorneys, among others.

Any relevant information to your business can be included in the appendix.

Chapter 3: Location, Location, Location

The location of your café can make or break your business. As such, when you plan your business, you must put effort into choosing the right location.

Your Café's Location

Your location will determine:

- *How many customers you'll have:* If your café is not in a suitable location, you will find it hard to get customers.

- *How many hours you'll work:* Your café's location will determine when you'll open and close your café. For instance, if you open a café in a rural area, you may end up opening late and closing early.

- *How much you'll charge for your products:* If your café is in an affluent location, you can set higher prices, but if it is in a less affluent place, you'll need to figure out how to offer low-priced products.

- *How much profit you'll make*: If you cannot afford to live near your café, you'll have to travel to and from the area, which costs money. It also costs money to transport your products to the café. That will cut into your profits. Since the location also affects pricing, this directly impacts your café's profitability.

As you can see, the location of your café is very significant. Thus, it would help if you took the time to select the site.

Factors to Consider When Selecting a Suitable Site

They include:

- **Visibility**

The first thing you need to consider when looking for a suitable location for your café is visibility. Your café must be visible from the road or in a high-traffic area. It would be hard for people passing by or driving by to see it if it is not visible. Also, you need to ensure the café has a visible sign. The sign will let people know your business type before they get near your café.

If your café is not visible from the road, you can look into using signage to direct customers to the café. For instance, you can place a sign or billboard directing people to your café in high-traffic areas.

- **Foot Traffic**

Look for a location that has high foot traffic volume. The more people pass near your café, the higher the potential for discovery. So, look for a busy shopping district.

It's also good to mention that, at times, people use different routes when they are heading to work or heading home. As such, you may notice high foot traffic volume at certain times and not others. The trick is to take advantage of the high volume. For instance, if the area has more people passing by in the evening, you can plan to increase the number of products you sell during that time.

- **Demographics**

Before choosing the location for your café, you need to study the surrounding area's demographics. The demographics will affect your menu, atmosphere, and pricing.

It would help if you looked at:

- *Proximity:* If your café is close to your customers, they can visit it more often since it is within their reach. But don't just look at the houses or businesses near you. If the building is somewhere people can stop by on their way to their destination of choice; you may still be able to get a lot of customers.

- *Age and income:* Look at the age of your potential customers. Younger people and families may have less disposable income than older adults. But they may be willing to spend more on special occasions such as date nights, birthdays, or celebrations.

- *Lifestyle*: How do the people in the surrounding area live their lives? Do they have kids? Are they professionals on the go? Do they hang out in groups or prefer sipping their coffee in solitude? If you know the lifestyle of your potential customers, you will be able to cater to their needs.

When looking at demographics, it is essential to note that while you don't have to cater to everyone's needs, ***people will spread the word about your business.*** As such, you'll find yourself attracting a particular group of people. For instance, if your café is child-friendly, you may have more families visiting your café. In this case, you need to determine how to accommodate child-free people. For instance, you can have them sit a little further away from tables with kids.

- **Competition**

As a café owner, you must recognize the difference between your competition and businesses you can piggyback on. *Your competition involves* local cafés, drive-thru shops, restaurants, gas stations, and chain store coffee shops. These businesses offer similar products to the ones you are offering, and as such, if the area you want to set up your café in has many such businesses, you may want to look at other locations.

Apart from your competition, it would help to *look at businesses you can benefit from*. These businesses complement your business. As such, their presence boosts your sales and vice-versa. Such businesses may include family fun venues, bookstores, libraries, and businesses with a wait. You can also look into starting a café near salons, pet groomers, car service stations, and transportation stations.

Your goal should be to find locations with businesses that can benefit from your business and vice-versa. You can work with other business owners to boost your sales.

- **Parking Availability**

When people visit a café, they do so because they are looking forward to something nice. This is why it is crucial to have adequate parking. If your customers struggle to park their cars, they won't like the experience, and their negative feelings will extend to your café.

Look into things like:

- **Security**: A parking lot should be well-lit with good surveillance cameras. It can also have security personnel to discourage criminal activity.

- *Accessibility*: Make sure the parking lot complies with accessibility standards. For instance, it should have ramps, curb cuts, and accessible routes for disabled customers.

- *Landscaping*: Landscaping is essential because it makes an impression on the type of people running the café business. So, ensure you have well-maintained plants and flowers and eliminate the weeds.

- *Cleanliness*: The parking lot should be clean. Remove any litter and debris that may discourage people from entering your café.

Your customers need to feel safe and significant when they visit your café. Remember, they will be spending money there, so the least you can do is ensure they have a pleasant experience.

- **Zoning Requirements and Permits**

Before deciding on a location, you must consider zoning requirements and permits. This is because streets are usually zoned for a particular reason. For instance, if you plan on roasting coffee beans, you must check if that area is zoned for roasting. If an area is not zoned for commercial use, you cannot have a café there.

Also, it would help if you considered upcoming developments when searching for an ideal location. If construction projects are in the area, check if they are residential or commercial and determine how they will influence your business.

- **Security**

Over the years, big business chains have closed shops in some areas due to rising crime and insecurity. The lack of security is something that also affects smaller businesses. You must deal with various challenges if your café is in a crime-prone area. For instance, you may have to cut back on the time you're open for business to limit the risk of being attacked or robbed. In this case, you may open later in the day and close early. This will limit the number of products you can sell.

You will also have to spend more money hiring security or getting an alarm and a burglary-proof system. Such things cost money.

But there's something else to note.

If your café's location is deemed unsafe by potential customers, they will not be too eager to visit your café because they fear for their safety. Or, they may only visit your café at certain times or in groups. So, evaluate your café location and imagine what it feels like to walk into and out of the café and towards the residential area. Some locations may seem ideal for doing business, but if they attract bad people, other people may shy away from them.

- **Infrastructure**

This is not something many café owners worry about, but it is something you still need to consider when choosing the location of your café. Look at the roads leading to your café. What happens to them when it rains or snows heavily? Are they still passable? If the roads don't have good drainage, people driving or walking to your café won't want to navigate them when the weather is terrible.

Also, consider what happens if your area suffers from a power blackout. Natural events such as hurricanes and storms may affect power and telecommunications. If a power blackout occurs, can you run your business? You may decide to close the shop during such events or plan to buy the necessary equipment to make you the only game in town when the weather is bad.

The trick is to think of what incidents can occur and what you can do about them. Once you find the perfect location, it is time to negotiate a deal with the landlord.

Negotiating Leases And Dealing With Landlords

Whatever you do, study your lease carefully before choosing your café's location. Remember, there are no standard leases. As such, landlords tend to list their requirements. As a potential tenant, you must also state what you want and require, hence the negotiating part.

Some things to discuss are:

- **Rent** – You need to discuss the rent base and security deposit.

- **Free Rent or Abatement** – This is how long you can stay rent-free. Depending on the landlord or area, it usually lasts 1 to 3 months.

- **Lease Term** – Discuss everything to do with the lease term, including commencement, lease expiration dates, rent start, and renewal. Also, discuss renewal and extension options. This may allow you to renew your lease with the set rates.

- **Tenant Improvement Allowance** – Find out how much it is, what it is for, and how it's paid.

- **Condition Received** – Before signing the lease, note down the condition of the space you've been given. Do a thorough research of the area and check to see if your findings are similar to what the landlord says about the space's condition. Also, determine who will be responsible for utilities, trash, repairs, and maintenance.

- **Exclusive Use** – If your landlord has several units to lease, you can take advantage of being the only one with a café idea to lock out future competition. This is by having a clause on exclusive use. Make the clause as broad as possible to enjoy exclusivity.

- **Signage** – Discuss the restrictions and responsibilities of putting up signs in and out of the café.

- **Discuss Rules for Defaults and Remedies.** It would be best if you also discussed any other restrictions the space comes with, including insurance, late fees, and the licenses and permits needed.

- **Right of First Refusal** – Find out if you can take the space next to yours if it is open. If you have the right of first refusal, your landlord must make you an offer before renting the place out to someone else.

- **Rules and Regulations** – Discuss which rules and regulations you or the landlord can set without informing the other party and which require discussion.

- **Relocation** – If the landlord has many units, find out if you can relocate to another unit if needed.

- **Subletting** – Can you sublease?

- **Remodeling and Renovations** – What happens when you want to remodel your café? Who is responsible for what?

- **_Smells and Sounds_** – There are usually restrictions against or protections for certain smells and sounds. Find out where your business stands.

- **_Hours of Operation_** – Find out if there is any restriction or requirements for things such as days, time, and holidays. When can you access the space?

As you can see, there are various things to consider when looking for an ideal location for your café.

So, what do you need to do?

- **Think of What You Want**

If you want something included in the lease, you must have it in writing. Verbal agreements will only take you so far. This is because your landlord or management can change. So, everything you agree on should be in your lease.

- **Know What Your Landlord Wants**

Listen carefully to what your landlord wants and tailor your negotiations to their needs. Remember, negotiations don't have to focus on money. They can focus on other things, which you have to study carefully to ensure they won't hamper your business.

- **Find the Middle Ground**

After determining what you need and what your landlord wants, you must find the middle ground. For instance, if you plan to put signs all over the building but the landlord doesn't want to damage their building, you can use temporary signs.

When negotiating, do so **intending to get a win-win scenario**. Start low, but do not make an insulting offer. Also, ensure you get all the details out in the open to avoid misunderstandings in the future.

Another thing you should do is **think outside the box when you're faced with a rule you don't like**. For instance, if the area is only accessible to the public during certain times, you can ask the landlord if you can prep for the day when the area is closed. This way, you'll be ready to serve the public immediately after the area opens.

All in all, you want to find a location that is suitable for you. Since you'll be spending many hours in the place, you should be happy to be there. Thus, find out what will make you happy and let the landlord know, and then see how you can make the location work for you as you work to build your brand.

Chapter 4: Crafting Your Cafe's Brand

Now that you've figured out your café's vision, determined your target market, and searched for the best location for your business, it is time to craft your café's brand. Your brand comprises *your café's identity, image, culture,* and *personality*. It is everything that goes into getting your business up and running and attracting and retaining customers.

Crafting a strong café brand is essential for:

- *Differentiation*

A well-defined brand does the vital job of setting your café apart from other cafés. It gives your café its unique identity; as such, your customers learn to recognize your brand by its **unique features**, enabling them to remember it.

To illustrate, think about the things you buy when you go shopping. No doubt, different companies are selling similar products. But you gravitate towards a particular product due to what sets it apart. For instance, you may look at **packaging, pricing,** and **quality** when shopping. Those things are part of its brand. They are what set it apart from similar products.

- *Attracting the right customers*

Your brand communicates your café's values, offerings, and personality. This means it has the power to attract customers who share the same vision and values. For instance, a family-friendly brand attracts customers with families because they have the same values. Customers attracted to your café because of its values become loyal to your brand simply because they resonate with what it stands for.

- ***Building trust***

Think of your brand as your word of honor. It tells people, 'I'm happy with what I do and the services I provide, and you won't be disappointed when you use my services and products.' Your brand lets people know what to expect from your products. So, they are assured of what they get whenever they buy from you. That fosters trust in your products.

- ***Emotional connection***

A well-crafted brand evokes an emotional connection with your customers. This is because they learn to associate it with certain feelings, memories, and experiences, turning the café into something dear and special to them. And because of that, they will develop a sense of loyalty and attachment to the café, making them repeat customers.

- ***Storytelling***

Your café brand tells the story of your café. It lets everyone know the café's origin, mission, and values. If you have a compelling narrative, your customers can engage with your café beyond the physical product. They will be invested in your café's journey, making them root for your success.

- ***Brand loyalty***

Brand loyalty is something you build when your customers visit your café repeatedly. When they first visit your café, they get a certain impression of your brand. That is, the products you sell and the experience they get. If the products and experience are good, they will return and become loyal customers.

- ***Word-of-mouth marketing***

When you have a strong brand, your customers will tell others about it. This is because sharing information with friends, family, and colleagues is only natural. This is why word-of-mouth advertising works so well. It brings new customers simply because someone they know had a good experience and told them about it.

- ***Consistency and recognition***

When you create a brand, you include certain things as part of your brand's identity. For instance, your café may be known for its fast service. As such, you'll want to continue living up to your brand's personality by ensuring your customers are served quickly. This creates consistency and makes your brand known for a particular thing.

Recognition is crucial, especially if there are other cafés near your café. Crafting a brand ensures that your café always stands out in a crowded market. It creates a unique identity that resonates with customers, setting the foundation for further growth.

To craft a strong brand, you should:

Build A Strong And Memorable Brand Identity

Your brand identity refers to how you want your café to be perceived.

To establish your brand identity:

- ***Identify the café's mission*** – Why is your café there? What is your café's goal? You need to have a mission statement that goes beyond making a profit.

- ***Establish your café's value proposition*** – You need something unique to offer your customers. This uniqueness should be highlighted in your marketing campaigns.

- *Create your café's visual identity* – You need to create a captivating logo for your café. Choose your color palettes wisely to create instantly recognizable visual elements. Remember to use consistent visuals across all platforms when creating your visual identity.

Always remember that a strong brand identity is essential in generating brand awareness. Thus, take your time to think of what you want before you create your mission statement and visual elements.

Here's something you should know.

When you first see your mission statement and your visuals, it is easy to get excited by what you see. But after some time, you may think of another statement or visual you like. If you'd already put your mark on all your products and online platforms, that would be a huge waste since you'll have to re-do everything again. And suppose your customers have already started associating your old visuals with your brand. In that case, they may end up heading to another café since a change in visuals normally indicates a change in management.

As such, it would be better to print out your logo and see how it would look in various circumstances. For instance, you can print the logo on the cups you plan on using or a t-shirt your employees will use. You can use that as your logo if you like what you see. Also, don't forget to do some research when looking for your logo and mission statement. Some companies tend to trademark such things. So, do your research to avoid legal trouble.

Develop Your Brand Image

As we've seen, your brand identity is how you want your café to be seen. Now, your brand image is how others perceive your café. It is your brand's reputation.

When you establish your café, people perceive it in a certain way. If you're not careful, your brand image will fail to match your identity. To illustrate, let's say you want your café to be seen as a 'modern café,' but you use old equipment and payment systems; your customers will wonder where the term 'modern' fits in.

To build a positive brand image:

- *Create high-quality products* – The type of products and services you offer will affect your brand image. If you plan on selling certain products, ensure you have the right products and prepare them properly. If your customers are assured of what they'll get from your café, they'll learn to trust your brand, and your reputation will improve.

- *Establish a social presence* – If you want people to visit your café, you must tell them you have a café. Spread awareness of your products and engage with your customers. You can do that through online platforms or traditional means of advertising. Take the initiative to introduce yourself to the other business owners in the neighborhood. You don't have to be buddies, but they do need to realize you're there and what you have to offer.

- *Invest in public relations* – This is where you intentionally raise awareness of your café through online blogs, trade publications, and news outlets.

When creating your brand image, pay attention to what others are saying about your brand. This way, you'll be able to correct any misinformation and work to clear your name in case of any accusations.

Create Your Brand Culture

Brand culture concerns your café's core values and how you reflect those values. Your brand's core values can be something like 'honesty' or 'reliability,' or you can decide to tackle moral issues or take political stances.

To establish your café's culture:

- **Define your values** – You need to define your values if you want your café to reflect those values.

- **State your values** – Let your customers know what you value. You can do this by stating your values clearly and discussing them on your website and social media platforms.

- **Walk the talk** – Don't claim to have specific values if you don't plan on living by them. For example, if you publicly support equal pay, you should pay your employees equally. This will show you stand by your values.

The thing to note about brand culture is that not everyone will like what you stand for. For example, if you serve vegan sandwiches, some customers may take issue with that, while others may have a problem with you if you serve meat sandwiches. So, you need to create your brand with the knowledge that you cannot please everyone, and that's alright.

This is also why you need to create a brand with the same values as yours. As a café owner, there are certain things you like and dislike. If you get into work to do things you don't like or believe in, you may dread going to work. For instance, let's say you are allergic to dogs and open a pet-friendly café. You'll have difficulty interacting with your customers, affecting your brand.

Culture is a way of life. Thus, signing onto a culture that poses great difficulties to you would be imprudent. In other words, don't claim to be something you're not to compete with your competitors. Instead, identify your values and make them part of your culture.

Cultivate Your Brand Personality

This refers to the human characteristics your café has. It is what helps you connect with your customers on an emotional level. When you develop a brand personality, your business becomes more relatable to your customers.

To develop a brand personality:

- **Know Your Customers**

As you know, one of the first things you need to do as a café owner is identify your target market. But it is not enough to establish who your customers are. It would be best if you tried to learn more about them. Find out what they're into and how they speak. This way, you'll find common ground when you communicate with them.

- **Engage With Your Customers**

Nowadays, social media has enabled brands to engage with their customers. However, many business owners don't see the need for a social media presence since they have a physical location to conduct their business. But you need to realize your customers are online. Thus, having a social media presence reminds them of your existence. It also helps you tell your café's story and showcase the daily or weekly specials or any new information or product you want your customers to know.

Social media also introduces you to potential customers and new business opportunities. For instance, someone in your area may learn about your café via social media, or someone hosting an event in your area may reach out to you to see if you can provide refreshments for the event. Such potential customers may ask questions on your social media platforms, and when you interact with them, other people will also get to know what you have to offer.

- **Develop a Consistent Brand Message**

Your brand personality needs to be consistent across all channels. For instance, if you choose to be funny and informal, you must be consistent online and offline. If you are funny and informal online but coldly professional offline, you will put off or confuse your customers because they already have certain expectations of you. So, create a consistent tone whenever you deal with your customers.

Also, it is important to remember your *café's concept* when you deal with your customers. For example, if you intend for your café to serve as the go-to social hub for your community, you'll be giving a different vibe if your café is always booked for private events. In this case, it is not wrong to host private events at your café, but don't pretend you are there for everyone in the community if you keep locking them out.

Another thing you should keep in mind as a brand owner is that every business has its brand. This identity forms early in your business, but you can learn from your mistakes and experiences and grow into a stronger brand. But to do that, you'll need to listen to your customers and make any necessary changes to better your brand.

If you make a mistake, own up to it, apologize, and learn to do better. While mistakes may cost you some sales, what you do afterward will determine whether your café survives. Remember, word of mouth is still a powerful tool. If you mistreat a customer, they will tell others about their experience. But if something happens and you take steps to make amends, your customers will see that what happened was not the norm, and this will change what they tell others.

So, always look for ways to build and maintain a strong brand name.

But there's something else you should note when it comes to brands.

It is not easy to knock down a strong brand.

If you've taken the time to know your customers and treat them well, they'll remember that, and if they hear something negative about your brand, they will question it because their experience was very different. So, building a strong brand serves as a protection for you. But you can't build a strong brand without awesome products. Let's take a look at how you can craft the perfect menu.

Chapter 5: The Perfect Menu

What is the perfect menu? The perfect menu is the menu that showcases your café in all its glory and enables you to make a profit. It complements your café's concept; as such, whoever visits your café feels as if they've got everything you promised them.

To create the perfect menu:

Design a Menu that Complements Your Café's Concept

When designing your menu, your café's concept must be in your mind. This is because your café should revolve around the experiences you want your customers to have.

For example, if your café is near the beach, you may offer cold drinks and sandwiches so that customers can quickly get something to eat and drink before returning to their fun. On the other hand, if your café is near a park, you may want to offer food and drinks so your customers can take their time to eat as they enjoy the view.

So, think of why your café exists and then create a menu that will complement your café's concept. So, for example, if your target customers are families, you will want to include kid menus. And if your target customers are busy office workers, you may want to include products they can eat relatively quickly or carry with them. This is why it is crucial to *learn your customers' preferences*. If you understand what they want, you can offer beverages and flavors they like.

In addition, designing a menu that complements your café's concept also means ensuring the menu descriptions, color scheme, menu photos, and menu design showcase your café's concept. For instance, you'll want to draw cartoon characters for kid menus and use bright colors and funny descriptions.

Also, remember how your customers see food and when they like flocking to your café? For instance, if they love eating breakfast and not just drinking coffee, you will want to incorporate bagels, croissants, and breakfast sandwiches into your menu.

Select High-Quality Ingredients

As a café owner, you'll want to select high-quality product ingredients. First, look at the products you'll be offering and where you can purchase the ingredients to make them.

Some common drinks are:

- Black coffee

- Latte/iced latte

- Espresso

- Cappuccino

- Americanos

- Café au lait

- Mochas

- Irish coffee

- Cold brew

- Vietnamese coffee

Apart from drinks, you may want to offer bread, pastries, sandwiches, salads, cakes, cookies, smoothies and sodas.

Often the simple ideas are the most successful. A great local café I know has a full range of coffee with all types of milk. The point of difference is there are only four dishes on the menu. It makes it easy for the chef and the team and also for the customers. It helps that the food is delicious as well!

With simplicity in mind work through the following.

- **List Down the Products You Want to Sell**

Which products do you want to sell? Take some time to brainstorm the products. Write down everything you may want to sell now and in the future. This list will help you know where you're starting from and what you hope to achieve shortly. It would be best if you also thought of products you can cross-sell. For example, if you're selling coffee beans, you should consider selling coffee cups. This way, if someone wants to make coffee at home, they can have some 'cute' cups.

- **List Down the Ingredients**

After listing down your products, you need to list down the ingredients that will be required to make a particular product. This step is significant as often café owners go over budget because they have to buy certain ingredients out of pocket or because they buy too much of a certain ingredient.

- **Source for Ingredients**

It is time to hit the market once you know your necessary ingredients. If you can, buy ingredients from as many vendors as possible. You can start by buying ingredients from reputable vendors and then look for smaller brands.

It would be best to remember that well-known brands are known for their products, but this does not mean they are better than lesser-known brands. As a café owner, you may be able to find better and cheaper products by looking into lesser-known brands.

- **Narrow Down Your Choices**

The next step is to narrow down your choices. Use the ingredients you've bought to make your products and decide which ingredients work best. This is the testing stage of your menu. You want to know which products to use and how much to use. So, measure everything and note down your results. Then, determine which products you'll use.

While it is tempting to stick to one vendor or one brand, you need to look for two or three vendors you can buy each ingredient from. This way, if the vendor is unavailable or raises their price too much, you can buy from another vendor instead of searching for a new one on short notice.

You can even make a practice of rotating the vendors every few months. Remember, these are the vendors you've chosen after extensive testing on their products. As such, you already know how best to mix their products. So, no matter which one you choose to buy from, the products you make will be of high quality, and you won't be tied down to one vendor.

Also, ensure you can find the products you want all year long. If you have a popular product, you want to ensure it is readily available. If a vendor can't provide the products when you need them, you have to see how to work around that.

- **Determine the Presentation**

How will you present your products? For instance, if you serve cappuccino, you may ask your customers if they want to add cinnamon to their drink. And if you serve sandwiches, you may want to offer things such as herbs or dressing. Such extra ingredients need to be accounted for. List them on your menu and ensure you get the best products. For instance, if you tell your customers you offer free sauce, don't offer a watered-down sauce that makes your customers feel bad instead of appreciated—also, study ways to plate the food instead of lumping everything together haphazardly. Remember, we live in the social media age. If you serve your customers food creatively, they may be inspired to take photos of it and post it to their social media accounts. This will result in a free advertisement for you!

Incorporate Diversity for Different Dietary Preferences

When you're in the food business, you'll be met with customers who cannot eat or drink some of the things you offer due to food allergies, intolerances, religious or ethical reasons, and special dietary requirements.

So, it would be best if you thought of how to accommodate dietary preferences like:

- Dairy-free and lactose-free

- Vegan

- Vegetarian

- Gluten-free and coeliac

- Paleo

- Tree nut and peanut allergies

- Fish and shellfish allergies

While it's natural to accommodate as many people as possible, you must be prudent when incorporating different dietary preferences if you don't want to go over your budget or waste ingredients.

You should:

- **Start Small**

Instead of dedicating many ingredients to different dietary preferences, you can start by offering products that accommodate dietary preferences and then scale up as demand rises. For instance, you can offer dairy-free options by using other forms of milk such as almond, soy, and oat milk.

The idea is to see how much the products are in demand and then increase the number of products you sell as demand increases.

- **Listen**

Another thing you should do is listen to your customers. What else are your customers asking for as they order the products on your menu? Train yourself and your staff to listen to the customer's feedback. This way, you can determine what else to add to the menu.

For instance, if many customers ask if you have bagels when you serve their coffee, you might want to add them to your menu. But if only one person asks for bagels, you may want to put the product on the back burner and wait for more feedback.

- **Advertise**

Potential customers may fail to visit your café because they are unaware that you offer alternatives. As such, it would be wise to advertise your products once you add them to your menu. Remember, the customers who asked for the products represent a larger group of people who may want your products. Thus, by letting people know you offer vegan, gluten-free, or non-dairy products, you give them a reason to visit your café.

- **Adapt What You Have**

Once you decide to accommodate different dietary preferences, you should look at what you already offer and determine if you can tweak the menu to accommodate the dietary preferences. For instance, when making things like cake or bread, you can determine which items you must exchange to meet the dietary requirement. This way, you won't have to create new menus from scratch each time you offer alternatives, and your customers will be able to feel included since you're offering similar products but with different ingredients.

- **Always Ask**

Before you sell any product to your customers, you need to ask about their dietary restrictions. This prompts your customers to let you know if they have any food restrictions, and it also allows their family and friends to know that your café offers alternative products. Once they have such information, they can tell their family and friends about the options, increasing your number of customers.

Offering dietary preferences should not be a burden. It should be part of your daily operations. So, make it a natural part of your café.

Price Your Products for Profitability

You cannot claim to have the perfect menu if the menu you offer can't allow you to make a profit. Remember, if you're not making a profit, you won't be able to operate your café much longer. This is why you must consider how much you'll spend selling your products. Many people in the food industry go for a 10% to 60% profit margin, but you can decide how much you need to make as a café owner.

But before you settle on a price, look at:

- **The Target Market**

Think of how many of your target customers can afford your products. If you set the price too high, your target customers won't be able to purchase your products frequently. So, if you plan to sell to college students, you must keep your prices low enough for them to return.

- **Your Competitors**

It would be best to examine how much your competitors charge for similar products. Don't focus on one product - look at their whole menu. This is because some café owners may sell one product at a lower price, but they can make up the difference by selling another product at a higher price. As such, if you only look at the price of one product, you may end up pricing your products too low.

Also, when researching your competitors, you may discover something you can use to market your products. For instance, if your competitors are selling lower quality products for lower prices, you can sell higher quality products and let your customers know your higher prices will be well worth it.

- **Expenses**

When calculating your prices, you must consider all your business's expenses. Look at overhead, inventory, cleaning, maintenance, rent, compensation, and benefits. Your products should allow you to cover all these costs and more. You can ask yourself if your money will allow you to retire and how long it would take. If it cannot, you must think of ways to profit more.

For instance, some café owners cross-sell other items to keep their food prices low. If you sell things like mugs and t-shirts, you may do enough business to keep your food and beverage prices low.

- **Inventory**

Check your inventory and determine the quality of your products. Suppose you have high-quality or rare products; factor that into the price. Let your customers know that they are supporting a specific cause. For instance, let your customers know if your coffee or food items are made from ethical and fair-trade products. This way, they won't mind paying a little more and come to trust your products and support your brand.

- **Environment**

Think of everything your café offers: Wi-Fi to music, a well-designed and decorated seating area, and top-notch service. These things need to factor into your prices. This is because they contribute to the experiences your customers will get. As such, you should be able to charge more if you've put a lot into making your café's environment as comfortable as possible for your customers.

You want a menu you're familiar with, one your customers will love, and one that will bring you profit. You will achieve the perfect menu if you can achieve those three things. This is because you can market your menu confidently if you know it. If you know what your customers want, you can sell to them and even suggest new products they may love to try. And lastly, if you research the ingredients, you'll be able to minimize loss and get good products without focusing too much on brand names. That is a recipe for success.

And once you have the perfect menu, you can look at the supplies and equipment you can use to bring your menu to life.

Chapter 6: Essential Equipment and Supplies

Do you know the equipment and supplies you need to start a café? Nothing is as disheartening as finding out you've run out of money but haven't gotten everything you need to run your café.

To illustrate, let's say you've bought coffee beans and food ingredients, and you're ready to open your café, but right after you open, you discover you haven't bought any sugar. You don't have any money left to spend on this valuable commodity. What would you do?

That one item can make your opening day go downhill very fast. And if you're not careful, you may discover that you don't have several items and supplies.

So, what can you do?

Identify the Necessary Café Equipment and Tools

First, consider every tool and equipment you may need in your café.

These include things such as:

- **Beverage Equipment**

Your café wouldn't be a café if you didn't have the equipment to make the coffee, espresso, and any other beverage you may want to offer.

Some things you may want to get include:

- Frappe and smoothie blenders

- Coffee roasters

- Air-pots, satellite servers, and decanter

- Coffee brewers

- Regular coffee grinder

- Espresso grinder

- Espresso machine

As you buy your equipment, you must pay attention to any specialty menus you might offer in your café. For instance, if you provide non-dairy drinks, you may want to acquire different equipment for those drinks to avoid cross-contamination.

- **Café Equipment**

The next thing you need to look for is the café tools and equipment you'll use to keep the café running in top form.

You can get:

- Display case

- Cooking equipment

- Ice machine

- Refrigerators

- Commercial dishwasher

- Espresso equipment cleaners

- Beverage equipment cleaning brushes

- Espresso machine maintenance kit

- Steam wand cleaners and milk frother

- Water filters for beverage equipment

- Espresso machine cleaning brushes

Think of the equipment you need, and then think of the cleaning tools you need to clean the equipment.

Cleaning is a huge part of running a café. This is because you will be using milk products or making fresh juices. If you don't clean your equipment thoroughly, you may mess up the fresh batch of food and beverages and stomp on food safety rules, which will shut you down before you can recoup your finances.

- **Barista Tools**

Barista tools help provide the finishing touches to your products. They elevate your products to the next level.

Some tools you need are:

- Espresso tampers

- Portion scales

- Syrup pumps

- Knock boxes

- Measuring cups and spoons

- Frothing thermometers

- Frothing pitchers

- Lemon wedge bags and tea ball infusers

Apart from the tools you need for making your beverages, it would be best to think of things you need to make it easier to prepare the foods you serve. For instance, you'll need baking and decoration equipment if baking cakes.

If you don't know much about barista or pastry chef tools, you must talk to an expert and the employee responsible for preparing the food. This is because some baristas and chefs prefer some tools over others. If the tools are in your price range, you should consider going with their preference.

- **Café Accessories**

When starting your café, you want to encourage your customers to stick around as they order their food and drinks. One way you can do that is by providing accessories they would love to use.

For instance, if they can sweeten their coffee to their liking, they'll be more comfortable taking it at the café.

- Teacups and coffee mugs

- Teapots

- Coffee filters

- Sugar pourers

- Espresso cups

- Creamers

When getting accessories, you need to think of **color schemes** and **sizes**. Look for accessories that match your café's concept.

Also, it is important to think about the accessories and their prices in relation to things such as **breakages** and **theft.** What happens if the accessories break? Or if some of them disappear? If you have ordered customized accessories, you'll want to replace them with similar products. So, make sure you can do that. In the case of theft or breakages, ensure you have the budget to replace the accessories on short notice.

When you take all those things into account, you may decide to go with cheaper accessories. But don't confuse cheap with cheap looking. You still have to select accessories that match the atmosphere you want to create.

- **Disposable Café Supplies**

Disposable supplies are great because they allow your customers to order drinks to-go. Also, if you don't have many dishwashers, you'll need to figure out a way to keep serving customers with the supplies you have.

Some supplies you should use include:

- Paper hot cups and lids

- Coffee to-go boxes

- Custom coffee sleeves

- Plastic cups and lids

- Straws and stirrers

- Take-out cup carriers

The thing to remember about disposable supplies is that you are using them to serve your customers. As such, they need to be suitable for the purpose. For instance, if you're serving hot beverages, your customers should be able to hold the cups in their hands without getting burnt.

- **Café Ingredients**

The ingredients you buy will depend on the food and beverages you want to sell in your café.

Some ingredients include:

- Foodstuff

- Sweeteners

- Flavoring syrups

- Hot chocolate

- Milk

- Coffee and espresso

- Tea bags or loose tea

- Chai

You must taste-test your ingredients extensively to know them as the back of your hand. Remember, manufacturers typically add an ingredient or a process to differentiate their products from other brands. This means that something like coffee will taste different depending on the roast. The same goes for other ingredients.

The next step is getting them once you figure out what you need.

Assess the Right Balance Between Affordability and Quality

As much as you may want to go out and get any equipment and supplies you may need, it would be best to consider some things before purchasing anything for your café.

It would be best if you looked at:

- **Assess Your Café's Space**

Before buying any equipment, you need to look at your space. If you have a small kitchen, for example, it would be imprudent to buy sizeable commercial kitchen equipment. Also, keep in mind that people are needed to operate the equipment. So, while it is possible to fit several pieces of equipment in a tiny space, you still need to make space for your employees to operate comfortably.

- **Look at Your Budget**

The next thing you should look at is your budget. You want to buy the best equipment you can with your money. And depending on your money, you may buy some things and get others later. You may also look into buying second-hand equipment or leasing equipment. Of course, this means considering all your options carefully so you can plan for long-term use of the equipment instead of paying less for something you'll need to replace soon.

- **Determine if It is Convenient**

Before you purchase a piece of equipment, you need to determine how easy it would be to use and clean it. If the equipment is complicated, you may need someone to teach you and your staff how to use it. If the equipment is hard to clean, you will have issues if you spend a lot of time cleaning it instead of doing other things.

After deciding on what to get, you need to refit your café. It would be best to determine what equipment goes where to create an efficient workflow.

Understand the Importance of Efficient Workflow in the Kitchen

An efficient workflow helps you:

- Save time

- Reduce workplace conflict

- Get your customer orders right

- Reduce waste

- Make more money

Given the importance of an efficient workflow, you must determine your café's workflow stages.

Common workflow stages are:

1. The Register Queue

Many people understand queues. As such, if they enter your café and find a queue, they can estimate the time it will take for them to be served based on the number of people in front of them.

If your customers spend longer than usual in the queue, you have a problem. The problem may be with the cashier or the barista. So, analyze the situation before you add more employees. For instance, if the barista looks bored, the person taking the orders may be too slow.

But don't be too quick to hire more people. Instead, check if you have the right employee for the right job. An employee may not be great at making beverages but may be excellent at taking orders. In this case, the issue of delays may be solved by assigning the right employee to the right task.

2. The Register

This is where the customer places an order with the cashier. Once the cashier collects the cash, he'll write down some remarks on an empty cup and then place the cup in the space between the register and the barista.

As you can imagine, this area must be large enough to fit several cups.

3. The Barista Wait-List

Every empty cup the cashier places between the register and the barista goes onto a waiting list. The cashier has to monitor the number of cups on the waitlist. If there are several cups in the area, they have to slow down taking the customers' orders, and if there is only one cup or none, the cashier needs to speed up. Once your staff members work together for some time, they will learn to understand each other's cues. For instance, the barista may signal the cashier that they need to slow down the orders if he feels overwhelmed at certain times.

4. The Barista

Once the cashier places down a cup, the barista picks it up, reads what it says, and proceeds to prepare the cup of coffee. The barista has to prepare the cups on a first-come, first-served basis. As such, it is essential to arrange the cups so the first customer can fulfill his order. Once the barista completes the order, they place the cup in another area. At this point, the barista normally calls the name written on the cup and then picks the next empty cup.

5. The Order Fulfilment

Once the order is ready, the barista calls out the customer's name, and the customer collects his cup on the counter. At this point, the customer studies their order to determine if it is correct. If there is a problem with the order, the barista has to take the cup back and start preparing the correct order before returning it to the customer.

The critical thing to remember is that you need to create an efficient workflow. There are two things you can do to create it. First, ***ensure your employees don't cross paths as they work***. This is because they disrupt their work rhythm every time they do, increasing the risk of accidents and cross-contamination.

Second, ***ensure the equipment is situated*** to allow your staff to move in one direction. For instance, the barista should not move to the left and right when preparing a cup of coffee. Instead, if moving to the right, they should encounter the equipment they need to use as they go, hence, the workflow stages.

Besides developing an efficient workflow, managing your inventory more effectively to enjoy tremendous success as a café owner would be best.

Let's see what this is about.

Manage Inventory and Order Supplies Effectively

A great workflow won't do you much good if you don't manage your inventory and order supplies effectively.

Inventory management is good because it:

- Prevents under-ordering

- Reduces food waste

- Deters theft

- Monitors your business health

As such, you need to:

- **Decide Who Will Do Inventory**

The first thing you should do is assign someone to do inventory. This is to reduce inconsistency. Also, delegating this task lets your employees know that checking inventory is essential to the café's success.

If you can afford to, you can have two employees checking inventory. This way, you can get more accurate numbers and make up for human error.

Another thing you need to decide is when you'll check inventory. For instance, you can choose a time of day when the café is not too busy.

Many café owners find it easier to check inventory after they stop serving customers or early in the morning before work starts. This is because it is easy to assume you have a specific product only for it to be used up by the end of the shift.

However, the important thing is to check the inventory at the same time each time.

- **Determine when to Place Orders**

Once you check your inventory, you must buy the supplies you run low on. Choose a specific time and a specific person who will place the orders. You can place the orders right before you close or once you open. Do it at a time when the café is quiet and do it regularly.

You may also want your employees to always ask for the freshest ingredients. If you sell ingredients close to the expiry date, you may end up using more money if you don't use them all by the time they expire. Remember, you're now a café owner. As such, while no one will raise an eyebrow if you use day-old ingredients in your home, people will get your business shut down if they discover you are using 'expired' ingredients, no matter how much you argue that the ingredients are still safe.

So, check the dates before your order.

- **Create an Order Guide**

By checking inventory and ordering supplies at a particular time, you will slowly learn to estimate how much product is sold and how many supplies you need to order. If you choose to buy in bulk, you must determine the expiry dates for the ingredients and how to store them safely to avoid wastage.

If you have seasonal products, ensure you know how many supplies you need for the season.

Always have an order guide with you when ordering supplies. For instance, you can list all the supplies you use in the café and then list which must be ordered. This will make sure you don't forget any supplies. Another good thing about the order guide is that you can indicate which items should be ordered in bulk and which expire quickly. Knowing when your employees can order an item and how much to order will make your life easier.

Also, it would be best to see if you can pair inventory with a task such as stock rotation. Normally, you must do a first-in-first-out stock rotation to ensure you use the supplies with the closer expiry date. If employees do that work, they can check inventory as they do.

- **Compare and Contrast**

When dealing with inventory, you need to compare the reports you get. This will help you notice the patterns that are forming. For instance, you may see a pattern during certain days, weeks, or months. For example, you may sell twice as much during days such as school events. If so, you'll quickly learn how to prepare for such dates and what to include in your menu to increase sales.

When it comes to supplies and equipment, it is essential to ensure you get the best value for your budget and keep accurate records to know when you need to buy more supplies or when equipment needs repair or an upgrade.

As we've said before, your budget may not allow you to get what you want right now. But, by starting with what you can afford and paying attention to their impact, you may decide which equipment you can upgrade and which you don't need. For instance, you may find out you need a better blender instead of buying a more expensive coffee grinder since more people are ordering juices.

So, buy what you can now and then start saving for better equipment while assessing their need as you work.

Now that you know the importance of a café's equipment and supplies, it is time to look at what you need to do to recruit your staff and manage your team.

Chapter 7: Recruiting and Managing Your Team

You already know that many people view their jobs in the food industry as temporary jobs or jobs meant for teens and people looking for part-time employment. As such, many employees don't stick around for long because they are looking to do something else or because the pay is not good.

As a café owner, you need to know how to get decent employees who can perform the duties enabling your café to profit.

You need to:

Hire the Right People to Fit Your Cafe's Culture and Vision

One important thing to note is that anyone can make a cup of coffee, but not everyone can make 100, 200, 300, 400, or 500 cups. As such, hiring people requires you to go beyond knowing how to make certain foods and drinks.

So, what qualities should you look for?

- Teachable

- Reliable

- Leader

- Motivated

- Team player

- Committed

- Organized

- Confident

- Enthusiastic

- Good people skills

Remember, there are certain skills you would want your barista to have. But not everyone you hire will experience working in a café. And there are times you may be better off not hiring someone with experience if they cannot work with others in your café. In other words, knowing what you're aiming for is essential.

You want to hire people who can develop skills such as:

- **Multi-Tasking**

Normally, baristas must speak to customers, accept payments, and make drinks simultaneously. These skills require multi-tasking, especially if they also have other duties. An employee who is only good at one thing won't be able to pitch in when you're understaffed.

- **Cash Management**

Your employees must understand how to use a cash register, manage cash, and make change. They should also learn how to use a point-of-sale system if they choose to use that instead of a cash register.

- **Teamwork**

When you have several employees, you need them to work together so that you can have quick and efficient service. Each employee must respect others and understand their roles and responsibilities and how they contribute to the café's success.

As a café owner, you'll especially want to be on the lookout for *'hazing'* *tactics*. If the older employees are forcing the newer employees to do all the work they don't want to do despite what they've been hired for, you'll have a high turnover, as no one wants to be treated unfairly. So, ensure fair division of labor.

- **Attention to Detail**

All your employees need to develop their attention to detail. This will help them do their work more effectively. For instance, when taking orders, they must pay attention to alterations such as non-dairy milk instead of dairy milk. Apart from paying attention to the products, the employees also need to pay attention to the tools and equipment in the café and anything else that may affect the café.

- **Knowledge of Coffee**

Everyone working in your café should be knowledgeable about the products you'll be selling in your café. For example, baristas must know how to prepare different coffee flavors without looking at recipes. If your employees know your products, they can make recommendations and answer customers' questions.

- **Customer Service**

Your staff will be interacting with customers from time to time, and as such, they need to know how to take orders, receive payments, and address any issues that may come up while serving customers.

Once you realize a potential employee has what you are looking for, you can give them an offer.

But there's one thing you need to understand.

An employee needs more than good qualities to work in a café. This is where training comes in.

Train Employees for Exceptional Customer Service

When an employee joins your café, you must teach them your work culture.

You should:

- **Lead by Example**

Your employees will copy what you do. As such, don't do anything you expect them not to do. For instance, if you wish them to dress a certain way, don't dress differently because you're the boss. Instead, follow the same dress code. This will show everyone that no one is above the rules.

- **Demonstrate**

A hands-on approach works well in a café. Remember, some employees may not know the coffee terms you use. If you show them how to use something like a frother and explain what you are doing, they'll remember it the next time they are asked to do the same task.

- **Communicate Clearly**

When communicating, you must consider how you want the employee to do the task. Here's the thing. If you ask an employee to make you a peanut butter and jelly sandwich, you will be surprised at how many ways people can make something that seems so obvious to you. That is because you are used to making the sandwich in a certain way, so you don't expect anyone to make it differently.

If you keep that in mind, you'll understand the need to spell out each process step by step to avoid confusion.

- **Observe**

The power of observation will be helpful when you want to train your employees. New employees can observe other employees to see how the work is done. Also, you can observe your employees to see how they are doing and where they need help. Let the employees know you're observing them to help them acclimate to their job and not criticize them.

- **Look at Skill Sets**

When training new employees, you need to note what the employees excel at. For example, an employee may excel at making drinks, while another may excel at customer service. If you notice that, you may want to train the employees more in the areas they excel in so they can be put to work immediately.

- **Cross-Train**

Employees working in a café can quit, call off, get sick, or take a leave of absence. When they do, you'll need your other employees to step up and cover the absent employee's duties. As such, you have to cross-train your employees, that is, train them to do other duties and take on new tasks.

- **Retrain**

Sometimes, you must upgrade your equipment and systems or add new products to your menu. At such times, you'll need to retrain your employees to be updated with the new way of doing things. Also, if an employee is taking shortcuts when using equipment, you may want to retrain them on the proper way to handle the equipment to avoid accidents.

- **Follow Up**

Once you hire and train your employees, you still need to follow up on how they are doing occasionally. For instance, you can set up monthly or weekly discussions to ensure everyone is on the same page. During such discussions, you can discuss the work standards and try to see if an employee needs help with their work.

Training your employees is to equip them with the knowledge and skills they need to do their work properly.

Create a Positive Work Environment and Foster Teamwork

You want your employees to work at their best and stick around, but for them to do that, they need a positive work environment.

You can create one if you:

- **Clarify Roles**

Your employees need to know what you expect them to do. You need to determine their job description, the tasks they're meant to do, and their responsibilities within your café. If you do this, you'll be able to ignite productivity and reduce conflict. You'll also avoid a scenario where one employee does so much while another has almost nothing to do.

- **Outline Expectations**

The next thing you need to do is let your employees know what you expect of them. It's not enough for them to only know what you expect them to do. You also have to tell them the standards they need to expire.

Some expectations include the following:

- *Attitude* – Your workplace needs to be a positive place. This means you and your employees need to maintain a positive attitude.

- *Cleanliness* – Your employees should keep their stations clean and keep themselves clean.

- *Dress code* – You must decide what you and your employees will wear during shifts.

- *Reliability* – Employees should learn that they need to be reliable. For example, if they are supposed to start working at a specific time, they must arrive on time.

- *Customer relations* – Your employees must know how to talk to and treat your customers.

If your employees know what is expected of them, they'll know which lines they should not cross, which will protect them and their fellow employees.

- **Reward Excellent Teamwork**

You can build camaraderie in your café by rewarding excellent teamwork. Let your employees know you appreciate what they've done, and if someone goes out of their way to help another employee, you should thank them, give them a gift card, or even give them a weekend off.

- **Encourage Feedback**

Every employee you hire has something to say. Letting them know you are open to hearing it is up to you. Request feedback from all your employees since employees play different roles. As such, one employee may have insights, and another one does not.

Also, remember to open various feedback channels. This is because some employees are comfortable speaking up one-on-one, but some may prefer an anonymous feedback box.

- **Don't Micromanage**

While you want to be around when your employee needs help, you shouldn't micromanage your employees. This is because micromanagement breeds mistrust. Your employees will always walk on eggshells, leading to high turnover rates. On the other hand, if you train your employees properly and give them room to do their work, they can shoulder their responsibilities and even make suggestions on how you can improve things.

- **Encourage Social Events**

Social connections are an excellent way to create a positive work environment. They impact your employees' mood, stress levels, and performance.

Some events you can curate include:

- Outings to events and local shows

- Hosting a potluck

- Team wellness challenge

- Celebrations for holidays or employee appreciation days

- Team building exercises

- Volunteering

Social events allow your employees to see each other in different settings. This helps them break down the communication barriers and learn to work closely as a team.

Your goal is to foster a positive environment by laying out the rules, listening to your employees, and providing them opportunities to grow closer as a team outside the work environment.

Handle HR Responsibilities and Employee Retention

Many people associate HR with layoffs, firings, and HR violations. But HR is so much more. As a café owner, you need to learn all the duties carried out by the Human Resources department to run your café successfully. This is especially so if you will be playing those roles yourself before you can hire someone else.

Some of the HR responsibilities include:

- **Recruit Potential Employees**

HR is responsible for recruiting potential employees. If you're playing this role, you must understand what your café needs regarding help. When you first start your café, you're unsure how well your café will do. As such, you may want to hire as few employees as possible. To begin with, you may want to hire a manager, a barista, and a pastry chef if you plan on selling pastries. But as the café grows, you need to analyze the work that goes on in the café and determine where you need help.

When recruiting candidates, you should not forget to reduce your workload. This is because there are laws safeguarding employees regarding the number of hours they should work. New café owners often don't apply such laws to themselves. Thus, they end up working long hours to the detriment of their health. So, if you're working 12 to 16 hours daily, you must figure out how to reduce your working hours to avoid burnout.

- **Hire the Right Employees**

One issue you'll experience when you tell people you're starting a café is that they will tell you about someone they know who a 'good fit' for your café would be. While you want to hire employees, you should be more interested in hiring the right employees. This means you need to arrange interviews for everyone you want to hire. Don't just hire someone because they've been recommended by someone you know.

Once you hire the candidates, you need to onboard them. Make sure they fill in the paperwork correctly and then do an employee orientation to teach them where everything is and how things work.

- **Process Payroll**

HR is responsible for processing payroll. This is an essential aspect of the bob because it involves calculating taxes and your employees' hours. It also consists of calculating raises and bonuses and reimbursing expenses.

You should not take this job lightly because any mistake may cost you considerably, especially if you make a mistake when filing taxes. And if you don't reimburse your employees for paying for things out of pocket, you will risk losing them because they will conclude you don't value them enough to give them their just due.

- **Update Policies**

As the months and years go by, you'll have to make policy changes to deal with the changes in your café. For instance, many businesses were forced to formulate new policies to keep their employees and customers safe during the pandemic. As HR, you must make official policy updates, so everyone knows what is expected of them. You should also suggest changes to a policy if the current policy no longer serves the interests of the café or the employees. This will create a more positive work environment and contribute to employee retention.

- **Take Disciplinary Actions**

There are times when you'll need to conduct disciplinary actions when an employee breaks the code of conduct you've set in place. If you navigate this duty properly, you will help the employee grow from the experience and become better. But if you navigate it inappropriately, you may lose a valuable employee.

To illustrate, let us say you have a system of warning employees up to 3 times before you fire them, and an employee has made a habit of coming late to work. You may give the employee an official warning and let him know he needs to change his ways. Or, you may explain why he needs to follow the rules and suggest what he can do to ensure he arrives at work on time. By understanding the need for the rule and getting advice on how he can manage his time properly, the employee may end up arriving on time and grow into a valuable employee.

Now, let's take a look at another scenario.

Suppose you have an employee who arrives five minutes late, but the employee catches up quickly, finishes his work on time, puts in overtime, and even works over the holidays and weekends when someone else cannot do so. In that case, you'll need to look at the situation closely and determine if giving that employee an official warning would be worth it despite the value he brings to your business.

- **Keep Employee Records**

HR is mandated by law to maintain employee records. Employee records contain personal details about the employee and any contact information they have in case something goes wrong. They are also helpful in identifying skill gaps. As such, you can analyze them to determine where you need help when hiring and the demographics of your staff members.

The employee records can also help you identify which employees would benefit from further training. Thus, instead of always looking outwards when you want to hire someone for a job opening, you can talk with your employees to find out if they are willing to train for the position. If your employees see an opportunity to improve their skills and pay, they will be likelier to stick around.

- **Conduct Benefit Analysis**

HR needs to stay on top of their game regarding salaries and benefits. If you conduct a benefit analysis, you can keep up to date with what others in your industries offer their employees and what you can do to sweeten the deal. For instance, your competitor may be offering lesser pay but better benefits. As a result, they may get the best candidates not because their pay is better but because they offer better benefits. By doing the analysis, you can see where to improve.

As always, keep the goal in mind. Your HR goal should be to hire and retain employees. If you keep that in mind, the things you do will be geared towards helping your employees thrive, and when your employees thrice, your business will thrive, too.

Now let's look at another issue café owners have to deal with.

Chapter 8: Navigating Legal and Regulatory Requirements

The legal side of business is something you cannot escape when you are a café owner. But while it may look overwhelming, you must get it right before you launch your business. This will prevent heartaches and legal trouble later on.

To stay up to date with the legal requirements, you need to:

Obtain the Necessary Permits and Licenses

- *Business license* – Cafés need licenses to operate in the country. You can get a business license in your local county or city's zoning office.

- *DBA (Doing Business As)* – This is the license required when one runs a business under another name other than its legal name.

- *Retail food service license* – A retail food service license allows you to directly sell things like coffee and various food products to your customers.

- *Resale license for sales tax* – Some states charge sales tax. You'll need a resale license if you live in such a state.

- *Sign permit* – If you want to put up any sign, you will need a sign permit. When getting this permit, look at the sizes of the permit covers since you can be sued if you put the wrong one.

- *Coffee shop insurance* – You need insurance to protect your business in case of injuries or property damage.

- ***Food handler's permit*** – This permit enables your staff to serve food to the customers.

- ***Building health permit*** – Your café may need a health inspection to prove that it is in sanitary condition if you want to serve food to your customers.

- ***Liquor license*** – If you plan to serve alcoholic beverages in your coffee shop, you will need a liquor license.

First, you must go to your local city zoning office and determine all the licenses and permits you need to run your business. Write them down, determine how much each will cost, and then acquire them individually.

Understand Food Safety and Health Regulations

Having the correct permits won't help if you cannot follow food safety and health regulations. Such laws protect consumers against illnesses brought about by eating unsafe foods.

Food safety laws usually cover the following:

- ***Proper cooking temperature*** – The right cooking temperature kills bacteria and prevents foodborne illnesses.

- ***Sanitation measures*** – Sanitation measures such as washing your hands in between handling vegetarian and non-vegetarian food products serve to prevent cross-contamination. Plus, washing your hands thoroughly before preparing or cooking food would be best.

- ***Employees and customers interaction*** – You must set rules regarding how employees handling food will interact with your customers. For instance, if you have a pastry chef, you may require him to wear a head cap to prevent hair from entering the food. Also, it would be best to implement a no-tolerance policy towards smoking in the kitchen. If an employee wants to smoke, he must do it outside a smoking zone.

- *Water and sewage disposal* – You need water to operate a café, and the water you use to prepare food should not be contaminated. Rather, it should be able to meet the safety standards for drinking water. It would be best to have floor drains in your kitchen to make it easier to dispose of liquid waste.

- *Pests and rodents* – Pests and rodents are a big no-no in a café. As such, you must dump garbage every night to prevent rodents from invading your dustbin. Also, seal small holes to prevent rats from entering your café and store food in sealed containers.

- *Design and operation of premises* – If you intend to store dried foodstuffs or frozen foods, you must have proper storage areas. For instance, you can have a storeroom for grains and cereals. Also, ensure your café has proper sewage disposal necessities and floor drains and that your employees can access clean water.

- *Preventing contamination* – To avoid contamination, your employees must adequately clean your tools, appliances, and equipment. It would be best if you also colored code things such as ramps and carts or any appliances you use to ensure you do not mix vegetarian and non-vegetarian foods.

- *Personal hygiene* – Personal hygiene is of utmost importance. If your staff needs to wear hand gloves, kitchen caps, or face shields, ensure they do so.

- ***Food worker illness*** – Employees who suffer from a contagious disease should not be at work. Give them some time off to recover before they can return to work.

Every country has its own rules regarding food safety and health regulations. For example, the USDA (United States Department of Agriculture) is responsible for formulating and issuing food safety and quality guidelines in America.

As a café owner, your job is to keep up to date with such guidelines to ensure that you are doing what you're supposed to.

Compliance with Employment Laws and Workplace Safety

If you follow the food safety and health regulations, you will be well on your way to making your workplace safe. But there are certain things you need to do if you want to be compliant with employment laws:

- **Get an EIN**

Your Employer Identification Number (EIN) works like your social security number. It is the number the IRS uses to identify your business and ensure it pays taxes. This number is free at the IRS website.

If you want to be an employer, you must get this number.

- **Register for State Taxes**

Your EIN enables you to register for employee-related State taxes such as unemployment insurance and employee withholding tax. You can register for this at the Secretary of State Website.

- **Don't Engage in Employee Misclassification**

There is a difference between independent contractors and employees. Typically, employees are compensated at an annual or monthly salary, hourly wages, other benefits, or various compensations, while independent contractors own and operate their businesses. They include people such as accountants, carpenters, and consultants.

If you hire someone to perform a specific task or complete a project, you may need to classify the person as an employee, depending on your control over them. If you misclassify the person, you will be in trouble with the IRS.

- **Confirm Work Eligibility**

Don't employ people if you are unsure they can work in the country. In the U.S., you need to fill out IRS Form I-9 and instruct your employees to provide the relevant documents to show that they are authorized to work in the country.

- **Sign the Employment Contract**

This is a binding agreement between you as an employer and the people you hire to work in your café.

An employment contract should cover issues such as:

- Starting salary

- Employee benefits

- Responsibilities associated with the role

- Termination rules

Some business owners would rather send formal job offer letters than employment contracts. In this case, the letters will serve as substitutes for the employment contracts and protect you and your employees in case of disputes.

- **Set Up Tax Withholding**

As an employer, you should familiarize yourself with IRS tax forms such as W-2 and W-4 since you must withhold State and Federal taxes from your staff's paychecks. You can do this yourself, but hiring an accountant as your business expands would be wise.

- **Review the Law and Stay Compliant**

Studying what the Department of Labor (DOL) says concerning workers' rights would be best. Some States require you to post the laws covering your industry in the workplace so that your employees can become well acquainted with them. The laws set by the DOL cover everything from hand washing to discriminatory laws. So, make sure you go over them to protect yourself.

Remember, laws are there to guide you and your employees. But you may lose your business over something small if you don't follow them.

- **Deal with Insurance and Liability Issues**

The availability of insurance is a game changer for a café owner. Running a café can be hectic. You'll deal with complex orders, morning rashes, and staffing issues. Your insurance cover can help you out in case of anything.

It would be best if you looked into:

- *General Liability Insurance*

This is the first policy you'll want to get. This is because it covers bodily injuries, property damage, and most liabilities of doing business involving customers consuming your products. For example, if a customer accuses your café of food poisoning or an employer spills food or drinks on a customer, you'll be covered under this insurance.

- **Business Property Insurance**

This is the type of cover you need if you own your building. This insurance will also cover the things your business owns, such as supplies and coffee makers inside your café. The great thing about this type of insurance is that it can be customized to suit you depending on whether you own or rent the space.

The policy covers theft, vandalism, fires, hurricanes, and tornadoes.

- **Cyber Coverage**

If you intend to use computers, you'll want cyber coverage. This type of coverage will cover cyber-attacks, data breaches, and ransomware. If you have this type of coverage and general liability, you'll have basic protections for your business.

- **Workers Compensation**

This type of coverage is often required by law to cover things such as medical bills for your staff if they get a workplace injury. Remember, if an employee gets hurt while working in your café, you'll need to pay their wages and medical bills while they can't work. If you're not prepared for that, you may use much money.

- **Employment Practices Liability Coverage**

When you have employees, you need to protect yourself. This is because whenever you hire or fire someone, you risk facing a harassment, retaliation, or discrimination lawsuit. Also, if you break any laws governing employment regulations, you may pay a large fine.

As a café owner, you should think of ways to get better coverage for your café.

For instance, you can:

- *Lower The Risk Of Liability Claims*

There are things you can do to lower the risk of liability claims. For example, you can install non-slip mats in slippery areas such as near doors, and ensure you include signs to let everyone know the floor is slippery. You can also see areas such as the parking lot and the store have proper maintenance. The idea is to limit how an employee or customer can get hurt.

- *Train Your Employees On Safety Protocols*

Another thing you can do to negotiate better coverage rates is train your employees properly. If your employees know how to do their work safely, they will be less likely to get hurt. For instance, you can teach them how to use the various cooking equipment and lift heavy items properly. You can also tell them what shoes or clothes to wear to prevent injuries.

If they can get certified from their safety training, the better for them and you since that will show that you are serious about training your employees to avoid accidents.

- ***Have Adequate Fire Protection***

Your café will be used for cooking. As such, you can get more favorable insurance coverage with adequate fire protection. You can get a sprinkler system, fire extinguishers, or ANSUL system to minimize fire risk and losses.

Insurance companies don't want to lose money. As such, the less likely you are to claim money from them, the better rates they will give you. Typically, the rates may get revised after several years. During that time, if something happens, you'll end up paying higher rates the next time the rates are reviewed. Thus, always be on top of health and safety issues.

Now that you know what to do to hire employees and keep safe, let us look at how you can attract customers.

Chapter 9: Marketing and Promotion Strategies

As you dip your feet into the world of cafés, you'd do well to understand that you're just starting. As such, you'll face start-up challenges and competition from other businesses offering food and drinks.

This is where marketing and promotion comes in.

When you market and promote your business, you enable it to stand out and be seen.

You should:

Develop a Comprehensive Marketing Plan for Your Café

The first thing you should know is that there is no one-size-fits-all when it comes to marketing your café. As such, you should be interested in customizing the strategies you learn for your own business.

Your marketing plan should have actions such as:

- Establish your financial and marketing goals.

- Research the market.

- Analyze your target market.

- Create a calendar that will mark the step-by-step activities you'll do concerning marketing your café to your target market.

- Create a strategy to retain your customers.

Up to this point, you should have already written your goals, researched your market, and determined who you should target as your customers based on the information you've gotten. So now, you just need to determine which marketing strategies to use and when you'll start using them.

Three strategies you can use are:

Harness The Power of Social Media and Online Presence

Social media and cafés make for a powerful duo. This is due to the visual aspect of this type of marketing. You can market your café on platforms like Facebook, TikTok, and Instagram.

Think of when you'll:

- Post photos of your café

- Share menu items

- Promote new products

- Announce any events held in your café

- Engage with your followers directly and answer any questions they have

- Share tutorials and behind-the-scenes look

These activities are meant to reinforce your brand. As such, make sure you name-drop your brand, use your logo and café's color scheme when you post anything on social media and use relevant hashtags to reach more people. This way, your social media followers will learn to associate the things you post with your brand.

Now, before you start posting on social media, you should know something:

- **You Don't Have to Post Everywhere**

Choosing a platform or two for your social media marketing is okay. Look for a platform your target customer frequents and another platform you can post on. For instance, if your customers frequent TikTok, you can use TikTok and Twitter(X) or TikTok and Instagram.

- **You Need to Post Consistently, Not Often**

There is a difference between posting frequently and posting consistently. Regarding social media marketing, you must consistently post to cement your brand. For instance, you can post once or twice a day or once a week. The important thing is to create a habit that will let your customers know when to expect your posts.

- **You Should Post In a Voice that Matches Your Brand**

As we've said before, your café's voice matters. If your café is fun and goofy, you should use that voice online and offline. If your café is sophisticated, you should show that in your posts by creating a picture of sophistication. If you use your voice, potential customers will know what to expect when they visit your café, and some will visit you because of the image you've put out.

- **You Need To Interact With People**

If you decide to use social media, you must set aside time to interact with the people commenting on your posts. For instance, you can decide to comment on the posts for 20 minutes. If you have an active platform, you may only need to wait a few minutes before you start commenting. But if your platform is inactive, you can comment on a few replies and then like some comments. This way, you'll encourage people to continue visiting your page.

- **You Should Post Various Media to Mix Things Up**

Think of ways to mix it up when you post on social media. For example, you can post memes, photos, videos, customer features, and events. But whatever you decide to do, don't do it to the detriment of your other tasks. Also, remember it may take some time to start seeing results, or your post may go viral. Prepare for both scenarios.

Social media marketing is excellent, but you must target it to the people in your vicinity if you intend to sell products in your café. So, make sure you don't post in vain.

Engage in Local Community Events and Partnerships

You want to build your café into a community hub to get a lot of traffic to the café.

Some things you can do are:

- **Buy From a Local Vendor**

Buying from local vendors is a great way to involve your business in the local community. Look at the ingredients and products you want to sell and determine if there is someone near you selling them, and then buy them from that person. Start by introducing yourself to the person, tell them you have a café, and ask if they have what you need.

The idea is to build connections.

- **Cross Market**

The connections you build with other vendors will help market your products. For instance, if you buy fruits from a local vendor, you can ask him to mention that to his customers and tell him you may have smoothies. This way, his customers would want to stop by your café since you already have something in common. In turn, you can tell your customers where to get fresh fruit.

Cross-marketing works well because it exposes your customers to other vendors' products and their customers to your products. For instance, if you sell coffee alone, you can cross-market with someone who sells bagels since coffee and bagels go well together. This produces a win-win situation where both vendors sell their products, and the customers buy what they want without struggling to find a shop that sells it.

- **Partner With Local Artists**

Don't just think of food products when you want to partner with others. Also, think of the things you can sell in your café and the activities you can include. For instance, if you partner with a local artist, you can showcase their piece on your walls. This will not only improve your café's décor but also serve to showcase local arts.

Another thing you can do is partner with the artist to create branded products. For instance, you can make ceramic mugs and t-shirt designs. This way, your customers will readily buy your products, knowing they contribute to the local arts.

- **Donate to Local Charities**

Local charities have their purpose in your community. You can support them by enabling your customers to donate at checkout or donate some of your products to them. Remember, if you're in the business of cooking food and making drinks, there are days when you won't be able to sell everything you make. Instead of allowing that food to go to waste, why not donate it to a local charity? This way, you'll get to help someone while developing a positive brand image.

Note: Don't wait until your business takes off to involve yourself in the community. Start small. Start with the things you can do and look for opportunities to join community events and connect with the members of your community.

Utilize Loyalty Programs and Customer Retention Techniques

Customer loyalty programs are designed to keep customers buying from you repeatedly. They help you retain customers. As a café owner, the first thing you should do is determine who you will reward. If you reward everyone every time they buy something from you, you'll sell at a loss, eating into your profits.

So, what should you do?

You should:

- **Study Your Customers**

Always keep in mind that loyalty programs are a form of reward. To reward someone, they have to do something to deserve that reward. You must study your customers to determine which deserves a reward.

You can reward your customers based on:

- *Loyalty over time* – You can reward customers who've stuck around for a long time. For instance, if a customer visits your café every month, you can give him the product for free every now and then or give them a free coupon to use whenever they want. Or, you can offer them discounts.

- *Customer profitability* – Some customers buy many products, bring in their friends or family, or tell others about your café. If you discover such customers, you may want to reward them for what they do.

- *Speed of payment* – If you have a system whereby repeat customers can pay for the products they buy later, you may want to reward those who pay their tab as soon as possible. This will encourage them to settle their bills on time and buy more from you.

- *Their ability to purchase new or more café products and services* – Some customers come into your café to buy coffee or their favorite pastry, but when they see something new, they want to try it or buy it. You can reward such customers by giving them some samples of the product. This way, they may be tempted to buy more of the products.

- *The volume of purchases* – If someone orders many products from your café in one go, you can reward them simply because of how many things they've bought. Such customers may not buy from you often, but if you show them you appreciate it when they do, they will likely buy from you again when they want more products.

The idea is to base the rewards on something tangible.

- **Set Your Goals**

Once you determine the reward parameters, you must set specific goals the customer must reach to be rewarded. The goals you select should be in line with the reward parameters. For instance, if you reward customers based on their loyalty over time, you must determine how much time qualifies someone for the reward. For example, you can reward a customer who has been coming in regularly for one month, three months, six months, or a year.

- **Set a Budget**

The next thing you need to do is set a budget. Here's the thing. It is very easy to go over budget to retain customers. You may have to use some money to retain customers, but you shouldn't use so much that you can no longer run your business.

Once you've set your budget, you must think of ways to reward your customers.

You can:

- ***Drop Hints of Gratitude***

The simplest thing you can do is tell your customers thank you when they buy from you. Your staff needs to learn how to do this. For instance, if they see someone who has returned to the café, they can show the person that they remember them by calling them by name and mentioning what they like.

At this point, you can give the person something extra to show you appreciate them returning to the café. For example, if you had cooked a batch of cookies you wanted to start selling, you could give them one.

- **Use Discounts**

The fastest way to get someone to buy from you again is to save them money. You can do this by **offering discounts or cashbacks**. For instance, you can give them a coupon once they reach a particular reward parameter and let them know when to use it so they don't miss out on the discounted product.

Alternatively, you can **give them a printout of an upcoming special offer** that offers them a certain percentage off when they buy certain products. Give them enough time to prepare their wallets so they don't miss out on the offer. For instance, you can inform them of the sale dates and when it ends. If your loyal customers know the date before other customers, they will feel appreciated.

Another idea is to **have a punch card with a certain amount of money**. For example, the punch card can have circles with a dollar or 50 cents. Every time the customer buys from you, you punch out the circles until they are all punched out. Once that is done, you can offer them a 5-dollar discount on their next purchase. The best thing about this method is that it encourages the customer to spend more for the reward.

- **Use Social Media**

Don't just reward customers for buying stuff. You can also reward them for promoting your café. For instance, you can offer free bagels to the first ten people who post an item they've bought from your café. Or, you can provide a special discount to the first 20 people who repost your promotional status on Facebook or give your social media followers a coupon deal.

The idea is to drive people to your café even as you reward them for their online work.

- ***Give Gifts for Referrals***

Your customers have people in their life they can introduce to your business. But they may need a push to do so. You can use referrals to get more customers. For instance, you can offer discounts to anyone who brings someone else to your café or gift them something to show your appreciation.

Since the customer already buys from you, they will appreciate something extra for doing something they likely would have done as time passes. But by telling them about your referral program, you incentivize them to bring in people sooner rather than later.

When you think about marketing and promoting your products, you always want to keep five things in mind:

- How to promote your products

- When to promote them

- Who to market them to

- How much money you'll spend

- How much time you'll spend on promoting the products

Never forget that you're in business to make profits. As a café owner, you may need to set aside some money to market your products and some cash to promote customer loyalty.

If you have both budgets, you won't spend so much time trying to keep your older customers happy and forget to attract new customers. Loyal customers are great, but you need new customers to expand your business. But on the other hand, you shouldn't spend so much time and money attracting new customers that you neglect your older customers. If you do that, your older customers will feel unappreciated, and they'll find someone who values them more.

So, plan wisely.

If you want to take a deep dive into marketing your café you can have a look at *Brewing Success: A Comprehensive Guide to Café Marketing*.

You can find Brewing Success here:

https://www.amazon.com/dp/B0CPJ8P7P6

Moving on, let us look at how you can deliver an outstanding customer experience to keep your customers returning.

Chapter 10: Delivering an Outstanding Customer Experience

What does your customer want?

You must put yourself in your customer's shoes to answer this question. Of course, when you enter a café, you're looking to fulfill a particular purpose. Some people go there **to get a cup of coffee, use the Wi-Fi, or find a quiet spot to do their job**. But there's something that keeps them coming back.

This is the experience they get from being in your café.

And,

To create an outstanding customer experience, you should:

Cultivate a Welcoming Atmosphere and Ambiance

An outstanding customer experience starts with finding the right atmosphere for your café. You want a place your customers would be happy to be in and comfortable enough to relax and order more than one cup of coffee.

To create such a space:

- **Provide Soft Seating** – The seating area needs to be comfortable and inviting. You can have some armchairs, couches and the traditional chairs and tables and let the customer choose where he'll be most comfortable.

- **Utilize Low Lighting** – If your café has harsh lighting, your customers won't be able to enjoy themselves, especially if the lighting is hurting their eyes. So, shield your customers from things like the sun's harsh glare.

- **Add Some Greenery** – Plants and flowers can spruce up your café. They create a sense of peace and tranquility that lets your customers relax and take their time.

- **Provide Mellow Melodies** – Soft music can help set the mood of your café. You can have soft jazz, instrumental, or classical songs. The idea is to play calming tunes that don't interfere with your customers' need for conversation.

Remember, the atmosphere sets your customers' mood. If uncomfortable being in your café, they'd want to order something they can take quickly and leave. The less time a customer spends in your café, the less time you have to tell him about all the other products and services you have in store for him.

So, work to create a great atmosphere.

Enhance Customer Service and Handling Feedback

There are several things you can do to enhance customer service and feedback.

These are:

- **Set Customer Service Standards**

You cannot claim to provide excellent customer service if you have no idea what type of service you want to offer in the first place. This means you need to decide your customer service standards.

Some things to consider are:

- The tone and language you and your employees will use to communicate with your customers. Remember, when interacting with your customers, you want to convey your values and service ethics. Depending on your target customer, you can use formal or informal language.

- Next, decide who will contact your customers when they enter your café. Is it the barista? Or, can someone else greet the customer and lead them to their seat? This exercise aims to ensure the customer feels welcomed by the first person interacting with them. If you know who that person is, you can keep things consistent.

- Provide the needed support to ensure high-quality customer service. For instance, if you expect your employees to keep things warm and friendly, don't overwhelm them with so much work that they can hardly muster up a smile when they greet customers. Also, don't expect your employees to deliver things you haven't given them. For example, if you want them to give your customers freebies, you must provide them.

- Ensure there are enough employees to serve your customers quickly and invest in technology that will enable faster service.

- Keep delivery timescales realistic. If you promise your customers something you cannot deliver, they will end up disappointed. For instance, don't tell them you'll deliver their food within seconds when it takes minutes to prepare. Be realistic.

All your employees should know what you expect of them when serving customers.

- **Seek and Promote Feedback**

It would be hard for you to deliver an outstanding customer experience if you don't know how to improve the awesome things you are already doing. Remember, as much as you may put yourself in your customers' shoes, you cannot fully anticipate your customers' needs and concerns. The only way to do that is by seeking and promoting feedback.

Your customers' feedback lets you know what you can improve on and what you're excelling at.

As such, you should:

- Let your customers know you would be glad to listen to their feedback. Sometimes, people don't speak up because they don't want to offer unsolicited advice. As such, if your customers know you welcome feedback and that you have different ways for them to provide feedback, they will be more open to offering feedback.

- Make it easy for your customers to provide feedback. For instance, you can give out a simple feedback form they can fill out within a few minutes and then give them an incentive to fill out the form or take a survey.

- Give your customers the platform to provide online reviews and provide testimonials. Customers who are rooting for you want you to succeed, and they want to play a small part in making it happen. When you allow them to talk about your products, they will buy into the product and feel proud about helping it improve due to their feedback.

The important thing about asking for feedback is not to pay lip service to your customers. Rather, it is to show them you are ***willing to listen*** *to them and consider whatever they tell you*. And while you may not implement everything they tell you, they should be able to see positive changes as the days go by.

When they see that, they'll know you'll always listen, even if you may not always act. Thus, they won't be afraid to speak up in the future, enabling you to continue enhancing the customer service experience.

- **Exceed Your Customers' Expectations**

You can enhance customer service by exceeding your customers' expectations. For example, if your customer buys four cookies, you can give them one cookie free. Or, if your customer buys some branded products from you, you can give them a thank you card and stickers.

But make no mistake.

Your customer already expects excellent service from you. For example, they expect you to treat them respectfully and fulfill their orders correctly and within a certain period. So, to exceed their expectations, you need to do something more.

Implement Effective Customer Engagement Strategies

Engaging with your customers is a great way to build a loyal customer base. Your customers need to get something more than the products you're selling for them to feel connected to you. If you're just selling them the products, they won't feel disloyal if they buy the same products from someone else because they have no reason to be loyal to you.

Thus, it would help to think of ways to connect with your customers. Some customer engagement strategies you can use are:

- **Fix Mistakes Right Away**

Sometimes, a customer will complain about their food or drink order; at such times, your best action would be to **_apologize and make it again_**. You can ask several questions to understand the heart of the complaint before fulfilling the order. This is to show your customers that you won't get angry because they have an issue. If your customers know you're approachable even when things go wrong, they will be more likely to talk to you when things go right.

Plus, while fixing the problem, you are gaining valuable insight that can help you improve your customer service.

- **Provide Table Service**

Your customers will adapt to the kind of service you provide them with. For instance, if you offer coffee to-go and have a seating area but only concentrate on fulfilling the orders of the people who buy their coffee to-go, the people seated may be forced to head over to the counter to ask about their order.

This puts them in a bad light because other customers may assume they are cutting the line. So, they'll look for another café that offers better table service next time. On the other hand, if you ensure that the people in the sitting area are served within an appropriate amount of time, the people buying the coffee to-go may be attracted to their table and may plan to take a seat the next time they're there. This, in turn, will allow them to buy more products.

But there's another reason you should provide excellent table service.

The people taking their coffee to-go don't have much time to chat because others are waiting in line behind them. Thus, your employees can't learn much about them and how they perceive your services. But the people sitting down may have a few minutes to sample your new products and give their opinions. As such, the excellent table service gives you more wiggle room to engage with your customers and build connections.

- **Hold Workshops at Your Café**

Sometimes, your customers wish to have a cup of coffee but can't get it right. Or, they may be unable to go to your café for some reason. As a café owner, you can bridge that gap by selling them coffee beans and holding workshops to teach them how to make their coffee from home.

Also, if you play your cards right, you'll help your customers appreciate all that goes into making the drinks and foods you make for them. Get your most experienced baristas and chefs to showcase each product-making step. As we've said before, everyone assumes they can work in a café because they can make one cup of coffee. But once your customers see the work it takes to feed hundreds of customers, they will gain a new appreciation for your work and turn them into loyal customers.

- **Have Themed Days**

Themed days are special because they bring people who have similar interests together. Think about it. When a customer stands in line, he doesn't know what the person in front of him likes apart from coffee or whatever product they buy. So, there is not much interaction they can do. But when you have a themed day, for instance, kids' day, pets' day, or watch marathon days, your customers get the excuse to interact, increasing engagement while giving them something fun to do.

- **Host Voting Events**

Voting events can bring excitement into your café because they make the customers feel included. For instance, you can host an event where customers try out several drinks and vote on which one should be included in the menu. Create buzz for the event and let your customers know when they will be held, and once the winner is announced, add the drink to the menu at a discounted price for a specific time. This way, your customers will associate the drink with their excitement when voting for it.

When you think of customer engagement, you should think of what you can do to get your customers comfortable enough to share their views and excited enough to bring others into your café.

Build a Loyal Customer Base and Create Brand Advocates

We've already seen ways in which you can build your customer base. But to achieve above-average success, you must tie your customer base to your brand awareness.

Think about it.

It is one thing for a customer to buy one product from you and another for the customer to tell ten other people about your brand. In the first instance, you have a loyal customer who will continue giving your café business. While that is important, there is much more that your customer can do for you.

Your customer can graduate from being loyal to a brand advocate. They can help you:

- Improve your sales

- Build trust with newer customers

- Foster customer loyalty

- Save money on marketing

- Break into new markets

- Increase customer engagement

- Boost brand awareness

The work of a brand advocate is to engage with your café and promote it to a larger market through positive reviews and word-of-mouth.

There are three types of brand advocates you will want to attract. These are:

1. Influencer Brand Advocate

Influencers are typically paid a certain amount or given certain products or perks to promote a product on their social networks.

They promote your café when they:

- Share discount codes and affiliate links

- Share your café's content with their followers

- Use your products to create sponsored content

- Promote contests, promotions, and giveaways

Today, influencers bring awareness to your brand, but it is up to you to know how to capitalize on that amplification. For instance, if you've paid an influencer to share your content, you should be ready with some contest or giveaway once some of their followers look you up. This way, you'll increase interest in your products instead of just getting clicks.

2. Customer Brand Advocate

You want your customers to be your greatest brand advocates. This is because they can reach more 'real' people. While most of them may not have a large following on social media, the people they interact with maybe people they know in real life. As such, if they tell them about your brand, they will be more likely to take action.

Customer brand advocates can:

- Write reviews

- Show what they have purchased from your café on their social networks

- Provide word-of-mouth referrals

- Post a link to your website or social networks

- Share your posts

The thing to understand is that your customers are connected to other people, and those other people are connected to other people. Thus, if you teach them to advocate for your brand, you will have many advocates – real people who use your products in real-time.

3. Employee Brand Advocate

When it comes to advocacy, don't forget your employees, as many small business owners tend to do. The people who work for you can be instrumental in taking your brand to greater heights.

They can:

- Let others know about your café's products and services

- Share what they do on social media – People love watching baristas and chefs work. If your employees can showcase their skills, encourage them to do it.

- Share café news, job openings, and new products on social media – Your employees can help you reach more people when you want to let people know about an event, new products, or job openings. The faster and wider the word spreads, the better for you because it means more people will know what your café is up to.

- Represent your café at professional or community events – If you have employees interested in things such as marathons, sports, and such things, you can sponsor them to enter events and represent your brand. This will bring more visibility to your brand and employees.

- Bring in customers from their network – You can give your employees coupons to give to their networks. The good thing about this is that it makes the employee look good and brings you more customers. If you're worried about employees misusing this system, you can limit the number of coupons or discounts they can give.

Remember, your employees know your café in and out. Thus, they already know what to sell to the people they approach. But to do that, **they must become part of your team**, not people who can be easily discarded. As such, reward them when they bring in more customers. Allow them to have employee discounts and treat them well so that they can take pride in what they do.

The bottom line is brand advocates are everywhere you look. But it starts with how you treat the people you interact with. Will you dismiss someone because they only buy the tiniest cup of coffee, or will you recognize their potential to tell others about your products and bring other customers in?

Your actions will determine how you see your customers and how well your café does.

Conclusion

Staring up a café is a journey that starts with a dream and ambition. But once that dream cements in your mind, you must take concrete steps to turn it into a living, breathing café. This requires passion, perseverance, and adaptability.

Remember, a dream is only too big when you don't take the first step. But each step you take afterward only brings you closer to your goal. So, instead of focusing on everything you must do to get going, focus on one action you can take today to realize your dream. When you complete that action, take the next action and mark off your checklist as you go. Before you know it, you'll have opening day jitters as you prepare to welcome your customers.

So, start now!

A note from the Author

Hello there!

I hope you've found "From Beans to Brew" to be a valuable companion on your cafe journey. As you embark on this exciting adventure, remember there will be highs and lows along the way. However, armed with the knowledge and insights shared in this book, you're equipped to navigate through any challenges that may arise.

Always remember the importance of thorough research and planning. Dive deep into understanding your market, your customers, and your unique value proposition. Develop a solid business plan that serves as your roadmap to success.

But amidst the hustle and bustle of entrepreneurship, remember to have fun! Running a cafe is a labor of love, and the passion and joy you bring to your work will resonate with your customers and keep them coming back for more.

Wishing you all the best on your cafe journey. Here's to creating memorable experiences, serving exceptional coffee, and building a thriving business that brings people together.

Happy brewing,

Sarah

Other books by Sarah:

From Beans to Brew: The Ultimate Guide to Starting and Running a Successful Café

https://www.amazon.com/dp/B0CLRK7511

Brewing Success : A Comprehensive Guide to Cafe Marketing

https://www.amazon.com/dp/B0CPJ8P7P6

From Beans to Brew (Companion Workbook): The Ultimate Guide to Starting and Running a Successful Café

https://www.amazon.com/dp/B0CW1G9YNY

From Bud to Bloom: A Comprehensive Guide to Starting and Running a Florist

https://www.amazon.com/dp/B0CVFWMSHN

Appendix:

Cafe Business Plan Worksheet

This worksheet is a guide to help you map out your cafe business plan, covering key aspects such as market analysis, marketing strategy, operations, finances, and risk management. Use it to organize your thoughts, set goals, and develop a roadmap for successfully launching and growing your cafe. Grab your notebook or computer and start making some notes about the following.

1. **Executive Summary:**

   - A brief overview of your cafe concept, target market, unique selling points, and financial projections.

2. **Business Description:**

   - Describe your cafe concept, including the type of cuisine, ambiance, and overall theme.

   - Define your target market demographics, including age, income level, and preferences.

   - Explain your cafe's unique selling points and how it stands out from competitors.

3. **Market Analysis:**

   - Conduct research on the local market, including demographics, competitors, and consumer trends.

   - Identify your cafe's strengths, weaknesses, opportunities, and threats (SWOT analysis).

- Analyze potential growth opportunities and market trends that could impact your cafe.

4. **Marketing Strategy:**

   - Define your marketing objectives, such as increasing brand awareness or attracting new customers.

   - Identify your target audience and develop customer personas based on their preferences and behaviors.

   - Outline your marketing tactics, including online and offline strategies, social media marketing, promotions, and partnerships.

   - Set a budget for your marketing activities and allocate resources accordingly.

5. **Operations Plan:**

   - Detail the day-to-day operations of your cafe, including opening hours, staffing requirements, and workflow.

   - Describe your menu offerings, pricing strategy, and suppliers.

   - Discuss the layout and design of your cafe space, including seating arrangements and decor.

   - Outline your inventory management and ordering processes.

6. **Financial Plan:**

   - Create a sales forecast based on projected sales volume and pricing.

- Estimate your startup costs, including equipment, renovations, permits, and licenses.

- Develop a budget for ongoing expenses, such as rent, utilities, payroll, and marketing.

- Determine your break-even point and projected profitability over the first few years of operation.

7. **Legal and Regulatory Considerations:**

- Research and comply with local regulations, health codes, and licensing requirements for operating a cafe.

- Obtain necessary permits and licenses, such as food service permits and business licenses.

- Consider legal structures such as a sole proprietorship, partnership, or corporation, and consult with legal professionals if necessary.

8. **Risk Management:**

- Identify potential risks and challenges impacting your cafe's success, such as market competition or supply chain disruptions.

- Develop contingency plans to mitigate risks, such as diversifying suppliers or implementing crisis communication strategies.

9. **Timeline:**

   - Create a timeline for launching your cafe, including key milestones and deadlines for each stage of the planning and implementation process.

10. **Monitoring and Evaluation:**

    - Establish metrics for measuring your cafe's success, such as sales growth, customer satisfaction, and profitability.

    - Monitor your progress against these metrics regularly and adjust your business plan as needed based on feedback and market changes.

11. **Additional Notes:**

    - Use this space to jot down any additional ideas, considerations, or tasks related to your cafe business plan.

Checklist for Opening Day Preparations

No.	FRONT-OF-HOUSE OPENING CHECKLIST	DONE
1.	Spot clean glass doors and windows – They need to be smudge-free.	
2.	Wipe down high-traffic areas such as door handles, seats, tabletops, and railings.	
3.	Check the bathroom and clean it if necessary.	
4.	Empty all the trash bins.	
5.	Clean the napkin stations and order area.	
6.	Put the sign on or turn on the open signage if you're using lights.	
7.	Unlock the café's front door.	
8.	You need to turn on a point-of-sale system if you're using it.	
9.	Make sure the register is set and confirm the cash amounts.	
No.	BACK-OF-HOUSE OPENING CHECKLIST	DONE
1.	Empty the dishwasher and make sure everything is ready to go.	
2.	Check the cleaning supplies and cleaning cloths and ensure your employees have enough supplies.	
3.	Check the surfaces and clean them where necessary.	
4.	Mop the floor.	

No.		DONE
5.	Preheat appliances such as stoves and ovens and other appliances you'll be using.	
6.	Restock your fridge and refill the milk and creamers.	
No.	**MANAGEMENT OPENING CHECKLIST**	**DONE**
1.	Walk around the café and check if the cleaning is being done.	
2.	Set the agenda for the staff meeting.	
3.	Review the staff schedule for the day.	
4.	Answer any emails and social media posts.	
5.	Organize the incoming deliveries.	
6.	Organize any upcoming projects, such as equipment fittings.	
7.	Pay any pending bills.	
No.	**FRONT-OF-HOUSE CLOSING FOR THE DAY CHECKLIST**	**DONE**
1.	Clean all the chairs and tables.	
2.	Place the chairs on the tables.	
3.	Sweep the floor.	
4.	Mop the floor.	
5.	Empty the iced tea and coffee makers and then clean them.	
6.	Clean the bathroom and check to see if it needs restocking.	
7.	Empty the trash cans and place the garbage in a dumpster.	

No.		DONE
8.	Close the cash register and then store the cash somewhere safe.	
No.	**BACK-OF-HOUSE CLOSING FOR THE DAY CHECKLIST**	**DONE**
1.	Sweep the kitchen floor.	
2.	Mop the kitchen floor.	
3.	Empty the kitchen trash and then take the trash to the dumpster.	
4.	Clean the cooking utensils.	
5.	Clean the employee bathroom and check if it needs restocking.	
6.	Check if the freezer, fridge, and walk-in doors are shut tight.	
7.	Turn off all appliances, including the stoves and ovens.	
8.	Check and audit refrigerator inventory. Place all older items at the front.	
No.	**MANAGEMENT CLOSING FOR THE DAY CHECKLIST**	**DONE**
1.	Perform an end-of-day cleaning walkthrough.	
2.	Make sure all the café's employees have clocked out.	
3.	Note down anything important or notable that happened in your manager logbook.	
4.	Answer the emails and social media posts.	
5.	Check the café's sales data and then make a report about the day's sales.	

6.	Make deposits.	
7.	Check all the exits and make sure they're locked. Lock the café and set the alarm before leaving.	

Resource List for Further Reading and Research

- Small Business Administration (SBA)

- IRS website for EINs

- Form 1-9 from the USCIS website

- W-4 Federal Tax Form

- W-2 Federal Tax Form

Made in the USA
Middletown, DE
15 June 2025

77042173R00080